What Does A
Real MAN Look Like?

By

ENRIQUE PASCAL

i

ENRIQUE PASCAL

What Does A Real MAN Look Like?

What Every Man And Woman Need To Know About True Manhood!

Enrique Pascal Communications

Copyright © 2013 by **ENRIQUE PASCAL**
All publishing rights belong exclusively to Enrique Pascal
Printed in the United States of America. All rights reserved under
International Copyright Law. Contents and/or cover may not be
reproduced in whole or in part in any form without the express
written consent of the publisher.

All Scripture quotations are taken from the Bible:
Amplified Version Copyright © 1954, 1958, 1962, 1964, 1965,
1987 by The Lockman Foundation
King James Version
New King James Version Copyright © 1982 by Thomas Nelson, Inc.
New Living Translation Copyright © 1996, 2004, 2007 by Tyndale
House Foundation.
New International Version®, NIV® Copyright © 1973, 1978, 1984
by Biblica, Inc.
English Standard Version Copyright © 2001 by Crossway Bibles, a
division of Good News Publishers

What Does A Real MAN Look Like?
What Every Man And Woman Need To Know About True
MANHOOD!
First Trade Edition – Published 2013
Printed in the United States by CreateSpace

ISBN13: 978-0-615-76704-8
ISBN10: 0615767044

Published in Richmond Virginia, by Enrique Pascal
Communications, Inc.
300 E. Grace St., Richmond, Va., 23219
www.enriquepascal.com

Thank You!

I would like to thank My Heavenly Father, Jesus my Lord and Savior, and the Holy Spirit my Counselor. Thanks for investing this amazing information in me and for allowing me to share it with the world. "You are the author and finisher of my faith!"

I would like to thank my wonderful wife, Katrina. You are my Proverbs 31 wife. Words cannot express how much I love and value you. Your dedication to me is truly appreciated. I love you!

I would like to thank my children, Marcella, Taylor, Antonio, Destinee, and Skyy. I thank God for blessing me with you guys. I love you all!

I would like to thank my father, Enrique Leon Ashby. I will always love and honor you!

I would like to thank my grandfather, George Joseph Pascal. Thanks for the start that you gave me. I love you!

I would like to thank my sisters, Yetira, Danitza, and Stephanie. God could not have blessed me with better sisters. I love you all!

I would like to thank my brother, Rogelio. I am proud to call you my brother. I love you!

I would like to thank Ray, Priscilla, Roberto, and Anna. I have learned so much from you guys throughout the years. I love you all!

I would like to thank my mother-in-law, Eunice Travers. Thanks for introducing me to Jesus. I love you!

I would like to thank my brother, Patrick. Thanks for all of the deposits that you have made in me throughout the years. This book is a partial return on your investment. I love you!

I would like to thank Al and Dereky Hagler. I truly appreciate the two of you. I love you both!

I would like to thank my brothers, Mario, Marcus, Quadree, Paul, Ken, Randy, Asante, Charles, and Wesley. I thank God for placing all of you in my life. I love you all!

I would like to thank Regina Baker and Dr. Taffy Wagner. I thank God for our connection. I love you both to life!

I would like to thank Howard Jones. Thanks for the counseling sessions and the seeds that you have planted into our lives. We love you!

I would like to thank a retired educator who served as the book editor and encourager, Martha Worsham. Thanks for helping me with this project. You are a blessing from God! I love you!

I would like to thank the Welch family, Mark, Vanessa, Marcus II, Isis, and Amir. Thanks for the encouragement. I love you guys. God bless you all!

I would like to thank Ron Hale. Ron, knowing you is truly a blessing. I pray that the good Lord continues to bless the works of your hands. I love you!

I would like to thank Paula and Virginia Pascal. The two of you will always live in my heart. I miss and love you both!

To our son Jeremiah, we miss and love you son! Your stay with us was short and yet very impactful.

Contents

Introduction   xi

Why I Wrote This Book   xiii

1   A Real Man Is a Just and Upright Man   1

2   A Real Man's Will Reflects His Woman's Best Interests   11

3   A Real Man Covers His Woman   21

4   A Real Man Is Not Concerned With the Public   29

5   A Real Man Respects His Woman   37

6   A Real Man Makes Good Decisions   45

7   A Real Man Understands the Strength in Quietness   59

8   A Real Man Keeps a Secret   67

9   A Real Man Is a Thinker   79

10   A Real Man Knows God   91

11   A Real Man Is a Dreamer   101

12   A Real Man Is Secure In His Identity   111

13   A Real Man Has No Fear   123

14   A Real Man Values What Most People Do Not Value   131

15   A Real Man Is Responsible   137

16   A Real Man Is Not Prideful   145

17   A Real Man Fulfills God's Will   153

18   A Real Man Obeys God   161

19   A Real Man Treats His Woman as His Equal   167

20   A Real Man Is Considerate   175

21   A Real Man Loves Without Limitations   181

22   Where Was The Beef?   191

23   What Determined Joseph and Mary's Success?   199

24   A Real Man Knows His Woman Well   207

25   A Real Man Is the Blender in His Blended Family   217

26   Which Man Will You Become?   225

27   Invitation   234

Introduction

Hello, my name is Enrique Pascal, and I am a retired champion runner. I never ran a marathon nor did I ever run for class president. But, I do remember running as a child during Field Day activities. My childhood sprints prepared me for the race that I ran for a good portion of my life. Actually, I was a winner at running from manhood. My existence was one continuous jog since it was similar to being on a treadmill. I was running, but I was not going anywhere. I appeared to be in great shape; however, the opposite happened to be the truth. My conditioning was terrible. The road to manhood left me breathless as it was hard, long, and frustrating. I began what seemed to be an endless journey as a boy, and then the man in me took over the baton in 2001. That year was monumental for me. For once in my life, I took a stance. Finally, I decided that the boy in me would no longer run the race for the man in me. Fortunately, I was not on this voyage by myself. I was introduced to "THE MAN JESUS" that year. Thank God! He coached and encouraged me with every stride I took.

I was born in Panama and raised by a single mother in the streets of Brooklyn, New York. I loved my mother, but her influence was no match for the misguided men I admired, music I listened to, and the movies I watched. These influences shaped and molded my thinking. They gave me the foundation for what I thought "A Real MAN" should look like.

During my life before meeting Jesus, I promoted parties and concerts in the world of Hip-Hop, and I became very prosperous at it. In 1993, I founded a promotion company named All-or-Nothing Productions handling several different types of entertainers. Also, I worked closely with Roc-A-Fella Records, a premiere recording company that was founded by Jay-Z and Damon Dash. Everything I experienced gave me a feeling of invincibility. Success can be harmful if there is no balance in your life. In February, 1999, I toured the country with the history making tour, The Hard Knock Life Tour. After visiting fifty five cities in ten weeks, I thought life could not get better. This feeling had me chasing fame and fortune. As a result, my sprint continued away from manhood and its responsibilities. The boy in me did not handle success appropriately; therefore, I became quite unstable. I was thriving in the career part of my life, but I was struggling in the other areas of my life. Since I was living on the edge, I was failing terribly in my marriage.

View the irony. I recall being told by countless people, "You are the man." These individuals obviously did not know me. They were making assumptions based on what they saw externally. I looked like the man according to perception, but I was far from the man. Honestly, my achievements in business along with the inappropriate role models injured me.

After years of bumps, scars, and bruises, I eventually discovered "THE" formula to true manhood. I would like to share this knowledge with the men who are trying to find themselves and with the ladies who are attempting to love these men.

Why I Wrote This Book

An email I received, and the circumstances I faced in my life inspired me to write this book. The email read:

"Hello, Enrique, my name is Brittany [name changed for privacy], and I am looking for real love. I am so hurt and frustrated. My last three relationships have sucked the life out of me. I am just sick, tired, and fed the heck up!!! One guy was married and never told me, the other ran up my credit cards, and the other is on the down low [living a gay lifestyle]. I had no idea. What does a real man look like? Please help me. I am a frustrated woman with a major issue. Brittany"

What Does A Real MAN Look Like? This question is the million dollar inquiry. Surprisingly, it is asked by as many men as women. Quite a few ladies are experiencing tremendous pain because they are involved with men who have no true sense of manhood. To make matters worse, society give us conflicting messages regarding this issue. The quest to discovering a real man can be dark and troubling.

What Does A Real MAN Look Like? Quite often, this question is answered with physical characteristics such as: tall, dark, handsome, blond hair, or blue eyes. This mindset is the major source of the problem. Society is so fascinated with the physical features of people that we overlook or pay very little attention to their emotional, mental, and spiritual state.

True beauty is on the inside of an individual, not on the outside. A person can have amazing looks and yet have a terrible heart. God is attracted to a certain type of man. "But the Lord said to Samuel, Look not on his appearance or at the height of his stature, for I have rejected him. For the Lord sees not as man sees; for man looks on the outward appearance, but the Lord looks on the heart" {1st Samuel 16:7AMP}. What kind of man attracts your attention?

What Does A Real MAN Look Like? This question echoed in my mind constantly, and my search for the answer steered me in the wrong direction. I was intrigued by drug dealers, womanizers, short-tempered men, selfish men, and men who utilized damaging words. I did not have any personal examples of a real man; therefore, I became the very person I admired. My life was a living hell, I was failing in all of my relationships, and I was on the verge of losing my marriage and family. The turmoil was too much for me to handle. As a result, I was depressed and haunted by thoughts of suicide. I was filled with constant frustration because I was trying to do the right thing, but I kept failing no matter how hard I tried.

It is difficult to know what is right if you were never introduced to the rules for good living. This statement is not an excuse by any means as I am not attempting to hide behind my faults. As a whole, my life was on the job training, and my wife was on the verge of saying those dreadful words, "You are fired." I should have been fired. I was doing a terrible job of being a responsible adult and a good husband. I struggled with my transformation; however, I was determined to transform into what I desperately needed to become – "A Real MAN."

I did not write this book to bash men or to pat myself on the back. In reality, I am very transparent regarding my own struggles with this issue. I love to help people, and I believe you can only help a person by exposing all of yourself – the good, the bad, and the ugly. With this understood, I wrote this book to shed light on a dark situation. Numerous people have tried to define a real man and have failed in their attempts. It is my desire to share with you important information which has radically changed my life for the better. I am excited for you because I believe this information is going to radically change your life for the better as well.

My journey led me to the greatest discovery in the world – the love of God. I cannot describe to you the freedom I felt once I discovered this amazing guide and example to true manhood. For the first time in my life, I surrendered to the Father who loves me more than I could ever imagine. His love is the reason why I made this life changing conversion, His love is the reason why I wrote this book, and His love is the reason why you are reading this book.

What Does A Real MAN Look Like? When I asked God this question, He revealed the answer to me in great depth and detail. He led me to Joseph, Jesus' earthly father. What an example of a real man. Joseph had to be an amazing man since God trusted him with the responsibility of fathering Jesus. I was moved and deeply inspired by Joseph's character. Are you ready to be moved and deeply inspired by Joseph's character? Are you ready to experience a transformation that will forever change your life for the better?

What Every Man And Woman Need To Know About True Manhood!

Connect With Me At:

Website: enriquepascal.com

Website: whatdoesarealmanlooklike.com

BlogTalkRadio: http://www.blogtalkradio.com/enriquepascal

Facebook: http://www.facebook.com/arealmanlooklike?fref=ts

Twitter: http://www.twitter.com/enrique_pascal

A Real Man Is a Just and Upright Man

Matthew 1:18-19 18 Now the birth of Jesus Christ took place under these circumstances: When His mother Mary had been promised in marriage to Joseph, before they came together, she was found to be pregnant {through the power} of the Holy Spirit. 19 And her {promised} husband Joseph, being a **just and upright man** and not willing to expose her publicly and to shame and disgrace her, decided to repudiate and dismiss {divorce} her quietly and secretly {Amplified Bible}.

A real man is a just and upright man. This statement simply means he is a man of good conduct. In this story, Joseph shows us we can behave respectfully despite the difficult situations we may be facing. He chose to do the right thing by maintaining his composure and not respond based on his emotions. He was scheduled to marry Mary only to discover she was pregnant, and the baby could not be his child. Still, he remained "a just and upright man." How many men do you know with this mentality? Imagine the inner battles he faced, and yet, he displayed a good attitude. There is never a justifiable reason to display bad conduct because unhealthy behaviors make matters worse. A real man never makes a situation worse since he is a problem solver.

Responding positively is a total contradiction to the way many men respond to obstacles today. We sometimes feel we are justified in behaving poorly because of a person's poor behavior towards us. This belief is harmful as nothing positive will ever come from it. God expects for us to display good conduct at all times. There are no excuses. For this reason, we have the profound example in the life of Joseph leading us the correct way. If Joseph could handle a situation as complex as his engagement to Mary, you can handle life's difficulties.

Joseph would have missed the golden opportunity to partake in a great act of God if he had conducted himself inappropriately. How many opportunities have you missed due to your improper actions? I have learned that the Lord utilizes tough events to bring out the very best in us, and He also uses testing trials to birth breakthroughs and miracles.

Because of Joseph's respectable approach, the Creator handpicked him to be Jesus' father. We can clearly see why Joseph's character played a major role in God's decision. God has also selected you to be a part of miracles and breakthroughs, but you will miss these occasions if your behavior is bad. Displaying positive thoughts and actions during troubling circumstances speaks to God, and it is a conversation He truly appreciates. It says, "I trust You are with me. I release all damaging feelings which may be attached to the hurtful events. I believe the end results will work out for my good. I will not become a victim of the upsetting issues. I will treat others the way I would like to be treated. I will not make matters worse. I will be part of the solution and not the problem." A real man speaks and most importantly thinks in this manner.

Corrupt actions imprison you. They hold you hostage to the hurt and pain that was inflicted. Cruel ways never benefit anyone no matter how justified you think they are. There are consequences attached to evil choices, and often, we do not consider the end results. Let us consider the repercussions Joseph would have faced if he had not accepted Mary's situation. It was the law to stone Mary to death as a punishment for adultery; therefore, Joseph would have been required to cast the first stone resulting in the murder of Mary and Jesus. If Joseph had responded negatively, it would have displeased the Creator and hindered the connection he had with Him. Is your performance pleasing to God or hindering your relationship with Him? Are your actions imprisoning you? Are your activities dangerous to others? What consequences are you facing because of your toxic performances? The questions I ask in this book are part of the healing and restoration process. Therefore, they must be answered truthfully. Do not rush through them, but spend time reflecting on the questions and your answers.

I have to be honest with you. I thought I had good reasons to display cruel behavior. I did not have a father figure in my life, I was poor, and I had to figure out the best ways to take care of my family at a very young age. The absence of my father was the missing piece of my life's puzzle. I felt rejected and incomplete, and I desperately wanted to fill the voids so I chose to fill the voids with harmful explosions. I believed these senseless acts were purging me of the anger, hurt, and pain that were consuming me. My condition worsened because of this ailing belief.

I wanted to be responsible and loving, although I displayed the total opposite. Responsibility is never accompanied by immoral actions. Bad behavior does not demonstrate what a real man looks like. Pressure or frustration is not an acceptable reason to exhibit terrible conduct.

Accepting responsibility for my actions was a major part of my recovery and rebuilding. I must admit that I was hurting the people who loved me and who I loved. I cannot hide behind excuses or justify my behavior. I behaved poorly. Hiding behind justifications or defending my foolishness is like giving me a license for my misconducts. In reality, excuses are a fine way to keep sinful attitudes alive. My dear friend, Regina Baker, shared this thought with me, "An excuse is a justification to make the soul feel good." Unhealthy thoughts and actions are like a flood which destroys everything in its sight. You need to immediately confront and correct anything you do unethically so it can no longer have

3

the power to live. Remember this truth, you will never overcome what you are not willing to confront.

Immaturity is displayed when a person demonstrates selfish choices. A real man is mature. Maturity has nothing to do with a person's age; however, it has everything to do with a person's character. I have seen adults act like children, and children act like adults. Have you ever seen a person behaving immaturely? What were you thinking as you watched them perform in this child-like manner? Have you ever asked yourself this question and felt somewhat embarrassed, "What was I thinking as I behaved that way?"

Reflecting is an effective practice as it allows you to take an intensive look at yourself, and by doing so, you will be able to make the necessary changes. It is like looking into a mirror and noticing your tie is crooked. What would you do if you realized your tie was crooked? Of course, you would fix it. This correction is what you should do when you are behaving improperly. I am not asking you to reflect on your poor behavior and choices for the purpose of adding guilt to your life. However, I am requesting this consideration for the sole purpose of instituting responsibility. It is not the Lord's desire for you to live with condemnation. On the other hand, it is His desire for you to take ownership of your decisions and actions. Ignoring your insensitive dealings or hoping they vanish is not the answer. This unrealistic way of thinking is like sweeping dirt under a rug. You may not see the mess, although the filthiness is still there. What happens if you continuously sweep filth underneath a rug? The grime will eventually reshape the rug as the lumps become more evident. That is why I am encouraging you to confront your issues. Once you face your struggles head on, you will flatten the lumps.

Many people are bent out of shape because they try to cover-up their sins. The constant sweeping of the dust under the rug is having a toll on them. It is easier for these people to ignore the truth than to confront their sinful ways. I have heard people say countless times, "The truth hurts." Here is a question for you: if the truth hurts, what does a lie feel like? Believing the truth hurts will hinder your relationships, including the one you have with God, your woman, family, and friends. The truth does not hurt, but "the Truth will set you free" {John 8:32AMP}. Therefore, accepting responsibility dissolves the lumps and evens everything out. Acceptance means you embrace the truth. As a matter of fact, cuddling with the "Truth" makes your crooked path straight.

Wicked dealings destroy the trust a person has in you. No relationship will benefit from this choice. Taking accountability for your unkind actions speaks to the Creator and others, it says, "I am willing to work at regaining your trust in me." The Lord can rely on an individual with honorable intentions. Would you be able to rely on someone with awful conduct?

A person's ways are always revealed so pay close attention to the little details, and do not dismiss or make excuses for them. Everything big was once small. A little blow up can become a big blow up, a little slap can develop into a big slap, and a little anger not controlled can turn into uncontrollable anger.

How do you manage yourself when you are in traffic? Are you easily agitated? What are the words you choose to use while you are angry? I heard Oprah Winfrey say this powerful statement, "When a person shows you who they are the first time, believe them." I totally agree. You are who you are regardless of the circumstances. Do not make excuses or play the blame game. Remember, accepting responsibility for your behavior is a key principle to restoring your link to God, your woman, and others.

5

This acceptance helps you to obtain peace. Ignoring your misconducts robs you of your peace. Doing the right thing replaces negativity with peace. The Creator does not want you to beat yourself up during this process, and neither do I. He desires for you to start with the man in the mirror and DEMAND for him to change his unpleasant ways.

Ladies, I wish I could promise you that your man will be transformed after he reads this book, but I cannot. Reading this book is part of the battle. The most important part of his journey will transpire when he decides to apply the principles which he has learned. Like the air he breathes, he has to desperately want the changes this book describes. I am a witness. Nothing permanently changed in my life until my desire for better engulfed me. Now, here is the great news, I can guarantee he will become the man the Lord intends for him to be if he wants it badly. Furthermore, his transformation depends on daily use of these teachings.

You should always be treated like a queen with respect. Never believe you deserve to be handled rudely as you are worthy of better treatment. Joseph did not treat Mary impolitely even with the difficult situations they faced. The average man today could not handle the conditions Joseph tackled during those days, and yet, he was labeled "a just and upright man." Your man has no excuses. His actions are a matter of his choices. If he did it or said it, he wanted to do it or say it. You did not make him do or say anything.

We are the owner of our responses. Blaming someone else for what we do will never help us to solve anything. You must hold your man accountable for his unacceptable deeds. Holding him accountable does not mean you become aggressive or act hostile towards him. If you do, you are copying his actions. By doing so, you will be giving him a way out, and the escape prohibits him from taking ownership of his misconduct. Therefore, he will focus his attention on your misbehavior instead of his misbehavior. Do not give him this opening. You shut the door on his unwise acts once you respond out of love. Taking this approach keeps the focus on him and the consequences of his actions. Suppose "Jonathan" spoke to you rudely, you should respond in a composed voice, "Jonathan, please do not speak to me that way. I really do not appreciate it, and I am not accepting this conduct from you. I believe you owe me an apology, and I am willing to accept it whenever you offer it to me. Thank you." The superior person is always quiet and calm.

Listen to your heart. Your heart knows if he is truly making a genuine effort to change his ways. Do not make excuses for him as there are none. You must be honest with yourself about the situation. Your honesty helps him with the conversion to real manhood. If you see he is making a heartfelt effort to become "a just and upright man," work with him. Encourage him with your words. Show him how much you value his efforts. Your encouragement is very helpful. Your expressions of praise will fuel and inspire him. Consider that his willingness to change does not mean he will not make mistakes. Even if he slips up, support him. Do not talk down to him, but rather talk up to him. Do not become frustrated by focusing on his current position. Keep your mind on the man who he will become. Be very patient along the way as this process requires much tolerance and love.

Here is a prayer for you: Father, teach "Jonathan" how to behave properly. Reveal to me what I should be doing to help him with his transformation. Touch his heart and remove all of the hurts and pains he may be holding onto. Give him the freedom he needs so he can become "a just and upright man." Help me with my reactions by letting me be the example of walking in Your light. I thank You in advance for our changes, in Jesus' name. Amen.

Reflection

Please get a notebook and dedicate it to the questions that I ask you in each chapter and for your comments as well. Please take the time to journal your questions and comments as a powerful way to track your progress. These moments are when you take the time to reflect on what you have learned in this chapter and express your thoughts. What did you learn from this chapter? Awful behavior is usually attached to a hurtful or painful moment in a person's life. What cruel or upsetting event is causing you to behave poorly? What should you do to recover from that aching moment? What are the steps you need to take to become a just and upright man? How badly do you desire to be a man of good character? What can your woman expect from you from this point forward regarding your attitude? The change you need will occur once you have a strong desire for it. How hungry are you for your transformation? Passionate cravings bring about true change.

There is nothing you can do to change your past; however, you do have full control of your present and future. Again, it is all a matter of choices. Move forward, do not get stuck in yesterday, and be encouraged as you reflect. A real man learns from his previous mistakes. A real man reflects on his former times, and as a result, makes better choices today to be successful tomorrow. Maintain your focus, and excellent conduct will become a part of your daily life. Count it as a blessing since you are able to look back on your earlier days and make the required adjustments for a victorious future. God is good!

Here is a confession for you to pray: I am a man of excellence, and I excel in all that I do. I think big, and I get big results because I serve a big God. I go the extra mile with joy to honor God and my woman. I am a man of high standards just like Joseph, and I will maintain my standards no matter the circumstances. I am an overcomer; therefore, I succeed in all that I do. Thank You, Father, for helping me with this transformation. I am a real man, and I will demonstrate this stance daily, in Jesus' name. Amen.

See if you remember what you read in this chapter.

When you are a just and upright man, you are a man of good

____ ____ ____ ____ ____ ____ ____.

A Real Man's Will Reflects His Woman's Best Interests

Matthew 1:18-19 18 Now the birth of Jesus Christ took place under these circumstances: When His mother Mary had been promised in marriage to Joseph, before they came together, she was found to be pregnant {through the power} of the Holy Spirit. 19 And her {promised} husband Joseph, being a just and upright man and **not willing** to expose her publicly and to shame and disgrace her, decided to repudiate and dismiss {divorce} her quietly and secretly {Amplified Bible}.

A real man's will reflects his woman's best interests. How was Joseph able to direct his will towards Mary's well-being while believing she had been unfaithful? He was a true giver. When your steps are ordered by giving, you are directed by the Giver Himself regardless of the circumstances. "If your enemy is hungry, feed him; if he is thirsty, give him something to drink. In doing this, you will heap burning coals on his head. Do not be overcome by evil, but overcome evil with good" {Romans 12:20-21NIV}. Amazing, when you are truly a giver, you display kindness to the highest degree. I must admit that I have struggled with this Scripture for quite some time; however, the struggle is now over.

It is plain to see that Joseph was passionate about giving. We know this belief to be true as his feelings were not fed by his anger, ego, or pride but rather by Mary's needs. There was nothing Mary needed more than protection; therefore, Joseph kept her safe by remaining silent. The story tells us he defended her by not "exposing her publicly and to shame and disgrace her, decided to repudiate and dismiss {divorce} her quietly and secretly." God desires for us to put the needs of our mate above our own needs. Our will has to line up with the Creator's will in order to follow His plan. Maintaining a healthy atmosphere is what a real man looks like and does.

You must give all of yourself in order for your nature to copy Joseph's nature. When you give all of yourself, you are giving freely. This unselfish act is exactly what Joseph did. Initially, he gave to Mary from his heart before he gave her anything tangible. When your contributions come from within, you are offering the perfect gift since your heart is the place where God has the most influence. "And I will give you a new heart, and I will put a new spirit in you. I will take out your stony, stubborn heart and give you a tender, responsive heart" {Ezekiel 36:26NLT}. Quite a few men are challenged when it comes to giving from their heart. As a youngster, I was taught by males to love with limitations. I was told, "If you give too much to a woman, she will always take advantage of you. Do not commit your all to a female. Do not let her know how you really feel about her. Hold back some of your feelings." Those discussions shaped and molded me as I was growing. Regretfully, I followed those instructions to the letter. Due to this poisonous way of thinking, my wife and I were constantly at odds with each other.

Joseph's actions and mine were totally opposite of each other when it came to a relationship with a mate. My marriage suffered because of this reckless choice. I was focusing on myself only. I did not protect my wife as Joseph protected Mary. How could I? I was too busy defending my warped mindset. I was a selfish man even though I thought I was a loving man. Do you see how confusing your life will become if you live according to the wrong beliefs?

Selfishness represents fear. A selfish man is afraid of losing something he values. His focus is on his potential loss instead of his family's gain. What would have happened to Mary and Jesus if Joseph concentrated on his loss instead of their gain? You will never lose if you are a giver. Joseph gave, and he did not lose. He gained from his giving. It is safe to say giving represents winning.

After I learned this principle and applied it, I won my wife's heart back. My actions regained her trust, and her appreciation unlocked her heart. Applying this belief transformed and totally changed our bond. I realized the more I gave her, the more I received from her. Like the sun, our marriage is now a cycle of continuous giving. At times, we both try to outperform each other with our giving, and we love it. I thank God I am free from this imprisonment. The pressure to be right is gone, and now, we are able to enjoy each other every day. Do not let pride get in the way of performing to this level. Pride hates the truth. Pride ignores wisdom. Pride insults others. Pride leads you in the wrong direction. Pride rejects valuable lessons.

I am not speaking about giving material items to your mate. I am speaking about committing all of yourself: emotionally, mentally, physically, and spiritually. Focusing on and strengthening these areas of your life will prove to be priceless. A donkey, house, or money would not have served Mary any purpose as she needed protection which Joseph gave her. When you are truly a giver, you offer what people need more so than what they want. Would you "give a man a fish or teach him how to fish?" There is a big difference between must have and like to have. In many places, we must have a car; however, it is not necessary to own a Mercedes-Benz.

Giving is not a deed that you should perform once in a while or whenever you feel like it. Giving is a deed that you should perform at all times. What would happen if the sun decided not to provide light? What would happen if the trees elected not to deliver oxygen? What would happen if the world chose to stop rotating? What would happen if the clouds decided to withhold rain? Do you see the importance of giving in abundance? Do you understand why generosity should not be an option but a mandatory duty for mankind?

Look at what the Lord states about giving, "In everything I have pointed out to you {by example} that, by working diligently in this manner, we ought to assist the weak, being mindful of the words of the Lord Jesus, how He Himself said, It is more blessed {makes one happier and more to be envied} to give than to receive" {Acts 20:35AMP}. Giving is certainly the way to shape and mold your will. You will be honoring God, your woman, and children by serving mankind.

You can never give too much. What would have happened if Joseph had given to Mary with margins? Giving in abundance shaped and molded his will towards serving God's purpose. There is great power in giving, but giving selfishly makes us powerless. That is why the Creator stated, "It is more blessed to give than to receive." The principle works because the more you provide to others, the more the Lord provides to you. You can never outperform God. For this reason, I am encouraging you to share in large amounts. The Father rewards us because He desires for us to be a blessing to as many people as possible. Do not be fearful that by giving abundantly you will find yourself in a place of shortage. There is no shortage when it comes to doing the right thing. The more love you give to people, the more love the Creator will deposit into your heart. The more patience you give to a person, the more patience the Lord will place into your heart. The more peace you give to an individual, the more peace the Father will put into your heart.

Look at it from this standpoint. When you give all of yourself, you are delivering God to everyone whom you meet. While you are offering all of yourself, you are offering hope to a hopeless society. Once you present your entire heart, you are giving people a chance at life. Joseph gave all of himself, and as a result of his actions, Mary and Jesus lived. Everything belongs to the Lord; therefore, what you are giving is more of Him. God has

14

entrusted you with the spirit of giving to align your will with His perfect plan. What are you doing with this gift? Are you giving the way Joseph gave, are you contributing out of selfishness, or are you refusing to give at all?

Do you know a person can give out of selfishness? There are two types of givers. First, a person can give with the wrong intentions such as to gain fame and popularity. The people who give in this manner are looking for self-seeking satisfaction. These individuals prefer to look good to others instead of looking good to the Creator. They give with limitations. They are not giving from their heart, but they are giving from their mind. These people spend time calculating when the biggest crowd would be present for the sake of feeding their ego. Is this mindset really giving? Of course not! We are to be a blessing to others as the Lord is always blessing us. God does not give to us based on the approval of people. In reality, you will find in the Bible that Jesus gave on many occasions without a crowd present. Is it better to supply a person's needs or feed your ego?

Secondly, you have to be a giver like Joseph who demonstrated compassionate giving. When you are a giver like Joseph, you give in secret, "not willing to expose her publicly." Once you give like Joseph, your heart rather than your mind directs you. Your giving is more impactful when you give from your heart. At that point, your ego is not a factor. The Creator loves it when you help people in private proving your will is in the right place. Giving in private means you are not giving for fame or popularity, but you are giving to satisfy the needs of someone else. Reflect on your intentions. When you give, why are you giving? Is it to shine light on you or is it to shine light on God?

Jesus said, "But when you pray, go into your {most} private room, and, closing the door, pray to your Father, Who is in secret;

and your Father, Who sees in secret, will reward you in the open" {Matthew 6:6AMP}. Giving in secret erases the ugly emotion of pride. Keep your spiritual eyes open. Pride is an emotion that creeps up on you and will overtake you if you are not watchful. Giving freely eliminates pride and aligns your will with God's will.

Like father, like Son. Jesus followed in the footsteps of Joseph as He gave even to those who did not deserve it. Even to His last breath, His thoughts were on you and me. Jesus' will was aimed towards our needs instead of the events before Him. You know you are in the right place when your attitude reproduces the characteristics of Jesus and Joseph. Living a sacrificial life benefits everyone, including you. You have to die to pride, selfishness, anger, ego, and resentment for these emotions tamper with God's will. It was the payment of Jesus to die for us as it was the payment of Joseph to conquer his negative emotions. As a result, Mary was able to live the life the Lord planned. Joseph's will was that of Jesus. I find this revelation to be truly amazing. The will of the father {Joseph} protected his Son's {Jesus} life, and the will of the Son {Jesus} granted His father {Joseph} eternal life. Jesus and Joseph's wills represents a cycle of unselfish giving.

It is the will and design of God for the godly woman to follow her godly man's lead. However, the woman will not follow her man's lead if he is not following God's lead. God is all about order. If your woman is not following you, check to see if you are following God. When your mindset is in alignment with God's will, your woman will be in alignment with you. The union will reflect you both going in the same direction for the advancement of the team. You are in the right lane when you are leading your woman and children to a reliable road towards the Creator's will. This alignment is what a real man looks like.

Ladies, lots of men are selfish because we have been taught to dominate and win at all cost. Embracing this teaching takes us out of God's will. One of the most difficult factors you will face in your relationship is the crooked will of your man. His strength of mind is an invisible force which has taken residence in the very core of his being. It was established in him long before the two of you met. Prayer is your greatest ally when it comes to this issue. Never underestimate the power of your prayers. Prayer leads and equips you. Prayer assists you in helping your man to discover what God's will is for his life. Remember, your man's selfish will is not physical, but it is a spiritual hole. That is why you should take this illness to the Spiritual Physician, Jesus. He has the cure. I am speaking from experience as Jesus came into my heart and performed major surgery on it. Now, my backbone is in alignment with God's will, and my choices display my wife and children's best interests. If the Lord changed me, He can certainly change your man. Thank You, Jesus! Do not give up. God is on your side. You and your man will stand victoriously.

Here is a prayer for you: Father, thanks for teaching "Carlos" the importance of giving. I am asking You to align "Carlos'" heart with Your heart. Teach him how to love me the way Joseph loved Mary. I am thankful that "Carlos'" will reflects Your will. I am also requesting that You strengthen me during this process. Make Your instructions plain to me so I may learn from this season of my life. Align my will with Your will as well. It is my desire to be in alignment with You and to please You. I am thankful that You heard this prayer, and that You always answer all of my prayers. I thank You in advance for "Carlos'" conversion and his proper placement in your Kingdom, in Jesus' name. Amen.

Reflection

Please take the time to journal your questions and comments as a powerful way to track your progress. These moments are when you take the time to reflect on what you have learned in this chapter and express your thoughts. What did you learn from this chapter? What do you need to do at this moment to align your will with God's will? Are you a selfish man? Are your selfish choices hindering your relationship? Does your woman lack your attention? Do you expect to receive from your woman what you are not giving to her? Are your children lacking your attention? How big of a giver are you? Are you able to give for the sake of others?

It is time for you to have a conversation with your woman if your will has harmed her. Genuinely apologize to her, and let her know that her comfort is of great importance to you. Inform her that you are going to protect her from this day forward and that your actions will signify giving in every sense of the word and not selfishness. "Actions speak louder than words." Your will has to reflect her well-being continuously; therefore, your actions ought to display thoughtfulness.

She may not believe you at first, but continue to reassure her that your will is no longer her enemy but her friend. This reassurance should not add pressure or frustration to you because these feelings do not display giving. If you feel or display any sort of frustration, your efforts are in vain and are not a genuine gift from the heart. If it is the real deal, it is not an act but something you just do. For example, you do not think about breathing. You just breathe. Once your will is in the right place, it is just that natural. Your persistence and constant dedication will eventually pay off. I am a living witness.

Here is a confession for you to pray: I am a man of excellence, and I excel in all that I do. I think big, and I get big results because I serve a big God. I go the extra mile with joy to honor God and my woman. I am a man of high standards just like Joseph, and I will maintain my standards no matter the circumstances. I am an overcomer; therefore, I succeed in all that I do. Thank You, Father, for helping me with this transformation. I am a real man, and I will demonstrate this stance daily, in Jesus' name. Amen.

See if you remember what you read in this chapter.

You must give _____ _____ _____ of yourself in order for your nature to copy Joseph's nature.

A Real Man Covers His Woman

Matthew 1:18-19 18 Now the birth of Jesus Christ took place under these circumstances: When His mother Mary had been promised in marriage to Joseph, before they came together, she was found to be pregnant {through the power} of the Holy Spirit. 19 And her {promised} husband Joseph, being a just and upright man and not willing to **expose her** publicly and to shame and disgrace her, decided to repudiate and dismiss {divorce} her quietly and secretly {Amplified Bible}.

A real man covers his woman. A real man is the same as a blanket who covers his woman from the cold. Joseph concealed Mary's pregnancy in order to protect her from a severe blizzard. The world can be a very cold and cruel place at times. Therefore, it is the responsibility of the man to protect his woman from the frostbite and harm. You need to embody warmth instead of coldness, and you must always cover your woman instead of harmfully exposing her to others. Covering her is demonstrated as you guard her from the adverse circumstances of life. Carrying out this task has nothing to do with your feelings or her actions. Carrying out this task is totally based on your willingness to be a just and upright man. While you are protecting your woman, you are fulfilling your duties as her covering. Defending and protecting his woman is what a real man looks like and does.

Ponder on this thought. If Joseph did not hide Mary's pregnancy, she would have been exposed to icy thoughts, cold stares, and fridge chatters. The exposure would have been damaging and deadly. Once a person's character is destroyed, it is very difficult to reestablish it. Are you showing warmth to your woman or are you as frigid as the Arctic? Have you wrongfully exposed her in any way? Women love to cuddle under a nice warm blanket as it makes them feel good. A man ought to create a cozy environment for his woman since a cold setting equals a cold relationship. How can you expect pleasantness if the surroundings are as frosty as Alaska? Exemplify a warmhearted, cuddly quilt, and you will reap the benefits.

A real man is like an umbrella who keeps his woman from the rain. The storm will come at some point; however, you have to be the buffer between your woman and the thunder {issues}. Reflect on how Joseph was the cushion between Mary and the potential flare-up. It is a sign of security for you to walk through the downpour without your woman. Your commitment to march solo during the rainfalls expresses your love for her. A real man guards over his woman by resembling an umbrella, but not just any umbrella, you must be a very big, strong, and sturdy umbrella. Your size, strength, and stability cover her from all angles and sustain her during any precipitations. Your leadership is all about safety and stability. Defense of his woman is what a real man looks like and does.

Imagine the rain, winds, and storm Mary would have faced if Joseph had not defended her. It is the nature of storms to cause major damages. Therefore, it must be the nature of the man to become the storm chaser. Chase away the rain clouds from your woman by serving as a very big, strong, and sturdy umbrella. However, pay attention to the reality that you cannot avoid all of the rain clouds. If you cannot ward off a bad experience that your lady may be facing, go through it with her every step of the way. She desires, needs, and deserves your escort. Be the symbol of a durable umbrella, and you will harvest the shining of the "Son."

A real man is the same as a tree who shelters his woman from the intense heat. You must give refuge to your woman from the extreme warmness of life {drama}. There is nothing like the shade of a tree on a hot, sunny day. Your woman may be in a setting with high temperatures, and yet, if you are like a tree, she is safeguarded from the intense heat. A real man sets the temperature in his relationship due to the stability he displays. Again, I am not saying your lady will not be exposed to life's tests and trials. However, when you symbolize a tree, your presence relaxes her. You will be like a cool breeze in the midst of the drama. Tranquility is what a real man looks like and gives to his woman.

Visualize a play featuring Joseph and Mary. Envision the traumatic commotion Mary would have performed if Joseph had not closed the curtains. Joseph considered the results and chose not to expose their circumstances. I believe this inner battle was one of his greatest challenges, and yet, he passed this test with flying colors. Bravo! I have given Joseph countless ovations for his stellar performance. Words cannot express how much I admire this man. He kept this drama a secret and "was not willing to expose her publicly." He did not complain or gossip to his family and friends. What was his outlet? Trusting in God was his outlet.

Joseph was willing to take the heat of the situation for the sake of keeping Mary cool. Joseph was the thermostat as he set the tone of the environment. The pressures did not control him, but he controlled the pressures. I learned a lot from his examples. If you set the temperature by sheltering your woman and remain the buffer between her and harm, the climate will respond to you. She will feel comfort regardless of the conditions. Symbolize a tree, and you will reap the gains of the cool breeze.

My character has grown due to these principles. I once was very cold as I exposed my wife to several storms {issues}. I kept constant heat {drama} in her life. I was a broken thermostat with the temperature gauge set too high. I can remember the endless frustrations I faced. I wanted her love, warmth, and respect, but I was not getting it nor was I freely giving it. I had to view matters differently and make the required changes in order to receive what I desired. I thank the Lord for change. Change is good.

I am now the protector of my wife in every sense of the word. Like a soldier at war, I serve, defend, and guard her. I exclude her from drama whenever possible. Her peace is extremely important to me. I have learned long ago that if she is not happy, I am not going to be happy. You know the saying, "Happy wife – happy life?" I am a witness to this belief. My life has become so much better since she knows I am passionate about her happiness. Stability is of great importance in a relationship, and I maintain it through the Word of God. This consideration of your woman's feelings is what a real man looks like and does.

If our child has a dilemma, I try my best to solve the problem first, and then, I inform my wife once it is resolved. The only alarm I want her to deal with is the one that goes off in the morning. Accommodate your lady whenever it is possible. The minute that you apply this approach, your woman is going to be grateful beyond your imagination. Living by these codes commands lots of consideration. Remember, it is all about defending your woman "by any means necessary." A real man considers not himself first but the loyalty he has for his woman. The Creator speaks of this loyalty in the Bible, and Jesus demonstrated this belief when He was crucified on the cross. "Husbands, love your wives, as Christ loved the church and gave Himself up for her" {Ephesians 5:25AMP}.

Ladies, the kind of man I am describing in this book is not a make-believe character out of a fairy tale. In reality, Joseph was a real man who lived in the worst circumstances, and he made the best of them. Do not settle for less because you feel as if this type of man does not exist. I am the product of Joseph's examples, and I truly believe there is a Joseph in every man. Your man has to strongly desire this experience in order to receive the benefits from it.

I had a burning desire to be identical to Joseph in character, even though, I was acting like a complete fool at times. I cannot describe the inner battles I faced when I behaved poorly. The guilt and shame was torture as they brought me to tears on countless days. I am not ashamed now to admit my faults. Overcoming my faults shaped and molded me into the person who I am today. Transparency opens the door to change.

It was a process for me, and it is going to be a process for your man as well. It demands relentless work to become a man like Joseph. The wonderful news is that the more your man implements these beliefs, the more emotional, mental, and spiritual endurance he is going to obtain. Once he maintains a strong focus on God's plan, he will become stronger and respond as Joseph did. These ethics will eventually become a part of him just like his eyes, arms, and legs are a part of him. I would not have believed years ago that I would become the man I am today. Be encouraged.

Again, remain prayerful, patient, and exhibit unconditional love. God is capable of changing your man if your man desires for this change to occur. Be a good judge of his intentions, but do not solely accept his words. His true conversion will be linked to convincing and consistent actions. Transformation is not without some form of on-going achievement. Be realistic, he will not become a Joseph overnight, but you should see his changes and sense them in your heart.

Be the example. My wife was mine. Display to your man the life you desire for him to live by your positive actions and words. When my wife responded with love, it played a major role in my transformation. She presented tolerance even when I was impatient. She showed understanding in spite of my inconsideration. The process will be challenging for you both. However, once it is mastered, you two will become a stronger team. Joseph and Mary were victorious, and you both will be also.

Here is a prayer for you: Father, help me to have the proper balance and staying power in this relationship. I really desire for "Derrick" to be transformed into a real man. Cover him with Your love and guidance as I cover him in my prayers. Teach him how to shelter me the way that Joseph sheltered Mary. I am thankful that "Derrick" sets a peaceful tone in our relationship and home. Reveal to me what I should be doing to assist "Derrick" with his makeover. I thank You in advance for mending all of the broken pieces, in Jesus' name. Amen.

Reflection

Please take the time to journal your questions and comments as a powerful way to track your progress. These moments are when you take the time to reflect on what you have learned in this chapter and express your thoughts. What did you learn from this chapter? Do you represent shelter in your relationship? Are you your woman's buffer? How important is her overall safety to you? What should you do to illustrate protection to her? Do others see you as her protector and defender?

Love to this magnitude speaks even when words are not spoken. You must be unshakable, have much patience, and strongly desire this relationship in order for it to become your reality. Change is a process which does not occur overnight, but you will achieve this makeover if your heart is in the right place. This sense of giving and protection is what a real man looks like and does.

Here is a confession for you to pray: I am a man of excellence, and I excel in all that I do. I think big, and I get big results because I serve a big God. I go the extra mile with joy to honor God and my woman. I am a man of high standards just like Joseph, and I will maintain my standards no matter the circumstances. I am an overcomer; therefore, I succeed in all that I do. Thank You, Father, for helping me with this transformation. I am a real man, and I will demonstrate this stance daily, in Jesus' name. Amen.

See if you remember what you read in this chapter.

What must you be like in order to protect your woman from the rain?

____ ____ ____ ____ ____ ____ ____ ____.

A Real Man Is Not Concerned With the Public

Matthew 1:18-19 18 Now the birth of Jesus Christ took place under these circumstances: When His mother Mary had been promised in marriage to Joseph, before they came together, she was found to be pregnant {through the power} of the Holy Spirit. 19 And her {promised} husband Joseph, being a just and upright man and not willing to expose her **publicly** and to shame and disgrace her, decided to repudiate and dismiss {divorce} her quietly and secretly {Amplified Bible}.

Joseph was "not willing to expose her publicly." We can learn from Joseph's example in two different ways. First, a real man is not concerned with the public's opinion. The judgment of others can steer you in the wrong direction. This misguidance is a flaw many men have. We permit the opinions of people to transport us down foolish paths. Joseph muted the voice of the public by not sharing his household business. His commitment to remain silent was wise. It is clear to see that God's opinion was the only one that mattered to him.

If you are busy pleasing people, it is extremely difficult to hear from the Lord. As Joseph knew, the Lord's truth is far more valuable than society's belief. Listening to many voices can be harmful, especially if you are dealing with stress. Who among us knows the complete truth about everything? When indecisions materialize, we should seek God's wisdom and not the community's estimation. Joseph took this route, and he proved to be sensible as he traveled on that road.

The thoughts of individuals should not influence you more than God's truth. Quite often, people form their views with little or no truth. They speedily construct their interpretations based on perception. "Looks can be deceiving." Things may appear to be one way and be the total opposite. Have you ever seen something from a distance only to see it differently from up close? Take a deeper look.

In this story, it appeared to Joseph that Mary had engaged in an affair and become pregnant; however, this appearance was far from the truth. If Joseph had condemned Mary, he would have displeased the Creator and gotten in the way of His perfect plan for redemption. Can you imagine the consequences he would have faced because of his actions? For this reason, I am suggesting for you to pray, wait for the answer, and then make your move. One ill-advised step will cause you to stumble and fall. The public is not responsible for your conclusions, but you are. You will be surprised to see how fast people disown you when things backfire.

The public's opinion is only an opinion. In comparison, their estimations are weightless on Heaven's scale. Indeed, Paradise's gauge always outweighs worldly views. Do you feel pressured to please the public? Are you concerned with how others perceive you to be? Who is your fuel? Is it the Lord or people? Do you seek God's wisdom before you make a decision? I cannot begin to tell you all of the mistakes I made in the past because I felt the need to please people. I once was easily moved by their opinions as I needed their thumbs up to validate me. Caring greatly about the thoughts of others hindered my association with God and my marriage. Insecurity is not what a real man looks like.

The Lord does not make His decisions based on the feelings of others. His rulings are founded on what He knows {truth}. "And they sent their disciples to him, along with the Herodians, saying, "Teacher, we know that you are true and teach the way of God truthfully, and you do not care about anyone's opinion, for you are not swayed by appearances" {Matthew 22:16ESV}. There is nothing like clarity when matters are vague. The path to understanding life's issues is in the Bible.

Think about the wasted time, the money you lost, and the pain you encountered due to an incorrect estimation. What decisions have you made based on an opinion that cost you a lot? What positions have you accepted that pointed you in the wrong direction? What lessons have you learned regarding the opinions of others? What are you going to do from this point forward to prevent history from repeating itself?

I am not saying to totally ignore the opinions of others, but I am stating that you should rest your options on the Word of God. Be open-minded. If someone shares a belief with you, make sure it is in alignment with the Creator's principles. "Without wise leadership, a nation falls; there is safety in having many advisers" {Proverbs 11:14NLT}. There is safety once your counsel is united with His will.

Secondly, by not exposing Mary publicly, we see the character of Joseph and how he dealt with these difficulties. He was not willing to share his personal affairs with others. Lots of men have failed at keeping their family business inside of the family, including me. We are so quick to grab the telephone and vent or gossip about our frustrations. Since these actions are drawn from negative emotions, our relationships suffer.

Think about the countless times that a person's private life is captured on television. To some degree, breakups and divorces have a public boxing match. From the starting bell, the media is in the midst of the battles. They are like judges at ringside keeping score. Each blow captures their attention while they eagerly anticipate the technical knockouts. No one wins. There are only losers. Joseph shows us how to deal with personal matters correctly within the walls of our home. Have you ever shared negative news about your woman only to wish you had not? Did it cause a wedge between her, your family, and friends? A real man must always protect his woman. Therefore, unconstructive conversations, harmful exposure, or character smearing is not a way to protect her.

Let us be honest, the public thrives on scandalous news and falls in love with lots of commotion. Why does bad news spread more quickly than good news? Do not be the carrier of negative broadcast, but instead be the transporter of positive reports. A positive story is what a real man uses to demonstrate his love for his woman.

The answers to all conflicts are internal not external. Internally is where you find the truth, and externally is where you find perception. Within your heart is the place where God has the most influence. Outwardly is where Satan has the most influence. The Creator works from the spirit {inside} while Satan works from the flesh {outside}. The Lord works by faith {on the inside}, and Satan works by the senses {on the outside}.

Resolving issues internally gives you the better options, and dealing with issues externally gives you the worse options. Joseph understood this truth. He was led by his heart and not by his mind. Understand that the spiritual heart and the human mind are always at war with each other. They never view circumstances the same way. It is vital for you to listen to your heart and also train your mind to follow your heart. Joseph's determination to do so honored the Lord's wishes. When a real man makes a decision, it is beneficial for everyone involved. A real man studies the full picture and not the parts which only profit him.

The key reason why you want to resolve your issues internally is that God speaks to our heart and not our senses or emotions. The heart is the place where the Lord communicates, dwells, and judges. "But the Lord said to Samuel, Look not on his appearance or at the height of his stature, for I have rejected him. For the Lord sees not as man sees; for man looks on the outward appearance, but the Lord looks on the heart" {1st Samuel 16:7AMP}.

Have you ever asked yourself how to know if the internal answer is the right one or not? You will know you have chosen the right answer by the amount of peace you feel. "Don't worry about anything; instead, pray about everything. Tell God what you need, and thank him for all he has done. Then you will experience God's peace, which exceeds anything we can understand. His peace will guard your hearts and minds as you live in Christ Jesus" {Philippians 4:6-7NLT}. God is the author of peace and not confusion, "For God is not the author of confusion, but of peace" {1st Corinthians 14:33KJV}. Never try to solve problems if your peace is absent, but rather wait for it to return to make your ruling.

Going for a long quiet walk is a great way to hear from the Lord. It is also a wonderful way to regain your composure. President Abraham Lincoln was faced with quite a few obstacles during his presidency, and he knew how to solve them. The remedies for his ordeals did not come from a doctor, but rather, they came from the Creator. He utilized nature and all of its beauties to still his mind as walked through the woods and waited for God's instructions. Remember, God is stability, and when you remain in His presence, frustrations are eliminated. If peace {the Lord} is absent, chaos {Satan} is present. Look at it from this viewpoint, no God, no peace! President Lincoln was an amazing problem solver. He knew God's truth is to rely on the internal instead of the external.

Conflicts are a part of life; however, you will solve them with the Creator's help. I believe problems and solutions appear simultaneously. The problem is that quite a few of us are trained to focus on the problems instead of the solutions. People are living outside of the Lord's will for this reason. I am not judging. I once lived by the rules of the outer domain instead of by the rules of the inner domain. For example, as a teenager in New York, I drank vodka at times before leaving for school. I wanted to fit in with my peers since their views meant more to me than my education. As a result, I lost out on a major part of my schooling due to those foolish choices.

It took me quite some time to learn how to live from within. My changes have worked wonders in my marriage. Living this way has strengthened my link to God; therefore, I am able to hear His voice clearly. As a result, my ability to make the right assessments and solve problems has greatly improved. What do you think would have happened if Joseph had dealt wrongly with conflict? What loss or pain have you experienced because you failed a testing trial? What should you have done to pass it? If you could change one thing about that particular situation, what would it be? What is hindering you from dealing with battles properly?

Ladies, you can learn a lot from this principle of letting God lead you to support your man. Cover your man and protect his character from the public. I am not saying to endure physical or emotional abuse. I am saying to resolve your problems quietly with God's guidance as Joseph did. The public does not understand your man. I have realized that people are quick to offer you their opinions but often would not follow the same thoughts if they were in your position.

My wife covered me despite of our problems. She knew I was going through a transformation as I was showing her signs of change. She had confidence in God and His ability. She believed He was working things out for us behind the scenes. The public's knowledge of our problems would have added to the stress we were facing and would have made matters worse. She chose to remain silent as Joseph did, and it worked. She was not willing to expose me publicly to shame and disgrace me. Her choice to work within our marriage granted the Lord access to our hearts, and He mended all of the broken pieces. Thank You, Jesus!

Make sure the advice you are getting concerning your relationship is good counsel. It must be based on the Word of God. The Creator's guidance is like a mirror which exposes everyone's flaws. It does not choose sides. It does not favor one person over the other. It favors the truth. It is the only way to honestly judge and cure any difficulties that you may be experiencing. You can seek God for His assistance by reading His word, prayer, and simply conversing with Him. He will never lead you in the wrong direction nor give you incorrect guidelines. He knows exactly what you need to do in order to get the results He desires for you both to have. Trust Him!

Here is a prayer for you: Father, thank You that "Larry" and I are focused on You and not the public. Teach us both how to cover each other by prayer. Connect us to the right people so that the advice we receive from them lines up with Your will. Thank You for always revealing the truth to us regarding all matters. I thank You in advance for giving us the plans which helps us to succeed in our relationship. I am grateful that we solve all issues within our home, in Jesus' name. Amen.

Reflection

Please take the time to journal your questions and comments as a powerful way to track your progress. These moments are when you take the time to reflect on what you have learned in this chapter and express your thoughts. What did you learn from this chapter? How do you feel about the opinions of others? What steps are you going to take to protect your woman from the public? What is more important to you – how you look to people or how your woman looks to them? How are you going to know if someone's opinion really matters?

Say this prayer daily: Father, You live in me, and You will never leave me in the dark. I thank You for blessing me with Your wisdom and the ability to remain calm. I am a problem solver, and from this day forward, I will search within for all answers. There is not a dilemma I cannot solve for You are my source of information, in Jesus' name. Amen.

Here is a confession for you to pray: I am a man of excellence, and I excel in all that I do. I think big, and I get big results because I serve a big God. I go the extra mile with joy to honor God and my woman. I am a man of high standards just like Joseph, and I will maintain my standards no matter the circumstances. I am an overcomer; therefore, I succeed in all that I do. Thank You, Father, for helping me with this transformation. I am a real man, and I will demonstrate this stance daily, in Jesus' name. Amen.

See if you remember what you read in this chapter.

The public is quick to form their opinion based on what?

_____ _____ _____ _____ _____ _____ _____ _____ _____ _____.

A Real Man Respects His Woman

Matthew 1:18-19 18 Now the birth of Jesus Christ took place under these circumstances: When His mother Mary had been promised in marriage to Joseph, before they came together, she was found to be pregnant {through the power} of the Holy Spirit. 19 And her {promised} husband Joseph, being a just and upright man and not willing to expose her publicly and **to shame and disgrace her**, decided to repudiate and dismiss {divorce} her quietly and secretly {Amplified Bible}.

A real man respects his woman regardless of the circumstances. He does not disgrace her, bring her shame, or tarnish her character. Instead, he honors her and views her as his queen. It is my belief that in a relationship a man needs respect more than anything else. Words cannot express how badly a man feels the moment he senses disrespect from his woman. In spite of that, men still disrespect their special woman. There is a double standard here, and it needs to be eliminated. If disrespect is not good for the man, it is definitely not good for the woman.

A real man knows the importance of showing respect to his woman and does not mind demonstrating it. It is an attractive sight for people to see. This attraction is contagious as others will hold her in high esteem due to your actions. Society admires people, places, and things of value. When you display respect towards your lady, others will see how much you cherish her, and they will think highly of her and your relationship.

Treasuring your relationship is not an act, but rather, it must be a part of your make-up. Demonstrating appreciation shows a mature and healthy relationship. It is safe to say Joseph was polite to Mary as he handled the situation appropriately. I am not saying he did not have challenges. What I am saying is he remained respectful despite of his feelings. A real man understands his attitude must be in the right place in order to appreciate his woman and show reverence to God.

Think about the frame of mind Joseph had to maintain in order to show kindness to Mary. Pause and enter into the thoughts of Joseph. What do you believe his thinking was during his greatest struggle? Is there ever a good reason for you to display rudeness? What mindset should you have in order to remain respectful? How important is respect to you?

Joseph understood a key principle. He knew you should treat people the way you would like to be treated. This next thought will help so many of us if we adopt and apply it to our lives. We should picture God in everyone. How would you treat people if you viewed them as an image of God? The truth is you will not view people as an image of God if you are looking at them with your natural eyes. We are imperfect beings. We all make mistakes. We all fall short of the expectations of others. Knowing that people make mistakes is not a reason for showing them disrespect.

You are not without fault. You will be in error. You will fall short of the expectations of others. How would you like to be treated? This key principle opens the door to a person's heart, mind, and hearing. If you choose not to use this vital principle, a person's heart, mind, and hearing will be closed. It is difficult to reopen a sealed heart, mind, and ear.

I have fought constant battles in my relationship regarding respect. My wife has an extremely strong personality, and she is very outspoken. This combination was not a good match for my out of control personality. I viewed her attitude as being disrespectful to me. What I viewed as disrespect was not disrespect at all, but rather, she was defending herself. My warped thinking saw her responses as challenging my manhood and authority. I was demanding respect, although I was not giving her the respect that I was demanding. For example, I embarrassed her one day in front of her clients. She made a statement that was contrary to what I had stated, and I was very aggressive in my response to her. I wanted her to agree with me, and she did not so I became very angry and ill-mannered. Everyone in the room felt the tension as my attitude silenced all voices. You could have heard a pin drop at that moment, and still, she remained respectful. I have since learned respect is not something you demand, but it is something you earn. Ego has a way of blinding a person.

This caveman mentality was readily accepted by me because of the movies, songs, and men who molded my reasoning as a child. My outlook has since changed, and I give respect to everyone regardless of how they may act or treat me. I have gained knowledge of the truth that I am responsible for me and me only, no one else. I cannot control what a person says or does. The realization of this reality has set me free and completely remolded my way of reasoning. This concept has worked wonders for me in every area of my life. Grab a hold of this very important statement. You will always lose whatever you do not protect and respect. Honor is magnetic. It attracts the right people to you, and dishonor repels the positive people in your life.

If you have a car and mistreat it, it will eventually not produce for you. If you do not change the oil, fuel it with the proper grade of gas, and perform the required maintenance, the vehicle will not function effectively. If you do not understand the benefit of people or things, abuse is inevitable. So many men are mistreating their woman. They put little or no care into their relationship and expect to receive one hundred percent in return. How can you expect to receive one hundred percent return if you are not investing one hundred percent? Does this thought even make sense to you?

If you give your woman one hundred percent respect, she is going to give that back to you in return. However, if you have tampered with her security, it is going to take some time to regain her trust. Disrespect causes separation in any association. I encourage you to continually make respectful deposits into her heart. Respect speaks loudly and clearly, as it says, "I honor you. I value our connection. I love you. You are important to me." Disrespect says the total opposite. You cannot remain discourteous and expect any sort of positive response from your partner. Do not expect for your union to grow if you refuse to feed it with love. Everything that has life must be feed. If not, it will ultimately die. Your relationship is alive. If you neglect to give it the proper nutrients, it is going to expire.

Respect is a key ingredient in a successful relationship. Spell the word "RESPECT" with these values in mind: Responding, Effectively, Sensibly, Patiently, Exhibiting, Consideration, and Thoughtfulness for others. Your woman and children will certainly appreciate you and all you have to offer once you are operating in this manner.

Ladies, I know you do not appreciate disrespect by any means; however, you must maintain your dignity if your man disrespects you. When you are upholding the crown on your head, your actions reveals the following statements to your man:

1.   You are showing your man and the devil that God is bigger than any offense.

2.   You are displaying to your man and the devil that your peace will not be stolen.

3.	You are a righteous example to your man.

4.	You are not becoming a victim of the situation.

5.	You are defusing the negativity.

6.	You are holding onto your joy.

7.	You are protecting your overall health.

My wife took this approach in dealing with me, and the fights and arguments began to cease. I had no one to challenge. Only a mad man or a fool would brawl and quarrel alone. Because of her new attitude, I felt like a complete fool. I needed the negative energy that she once gave me to keep the disrespect going. Her queenly stance did not allow her to fuel my disrespectful ways any longer. You are a queen, and you must stay on your throne wearing your crown. Disrespect robs you of the queen's duty, throne, and crown. Remain polite in spite of your king's actions.

Yes, your man is a king, although he may not be acting as one. Staying on your throne helps him to reclaim his throne. You both cannot abandon the thrones. If you do, who represents royalty? At times, he may forget he is an emperor. Let me encourage you to demonstrate and remind him who he is by remaining noble. As you take this route, your position of royalty is demonstrated to your leader. You will be surprised how the Lord will utilize you to bring about a positive change in his life. The Creator has utilized my wife in so many ways. When I was not listening to Him, she became His mouth piece. He will do the same for you, but you have to remain on your throne expressing your queen mentality. Your royal approach is needed. It is going to serve as a constant reminder that you both are a royal family. Your devoted politeness is very much a necessity.

Express to your man that he is your emperor, and you are his empress. Communicate to him that the relationship is the kingdom which you both have to protect. Convey to him that the empire {bond} is protected when you both are demonstrating respect to God and each other. Say to him, the estate {home} is divided if disrespect is alive. Advise him of this truth, "A kingdom divided by civil war will collapse. Similarly, a family splintered by feuding will fall apart" {Mark 3:24-25NLT}. Also, constantly tell yourself that you are a queen and that the circumstances of life will never dethrone you. Keep your head up.

Speak to the king in your man and not the fool in him. The person you communicate to will be the one who responds. You cannot speak to the clown and expect for the leader to reply. You must address the king so that the jester will have no place. State these encouraging words to him, "There is a king on the inside of you, and I will not disrespect our bond. I am honoring my emperor. I am your queen, and I desire to be treated as such. Let us rule our kingdom {relationship} together with respect, love, and dignity." Watch how this approach works for you.

Here is a prayer for you: Father, elevate my level of respect for "Marcus." Give me the words to inspire him towards change. Give me the eyes to see him as you see him. Teach me how to acknowledge and honor the king in him. Also, teach "Marcus" how to acknowledge and honor the queen in me. I am thankful that "Marcus" respects me as Joseph respected Mary. Strengthen us as we go through this transformation together. Guide us both towards respect, honor, and love, in Jesus' name. Amen.

Reflection

Please take the time to journal your questions and comments as a powerful way to track your progress. These moments are when you take the time to reflect on what you have learned in this chapter and express your thoughts. What did you learn from this chapter? Do you respect your woman? How do you display the respect that you have for her? Do you need to make a sincere apology to her for your disrespectful communications or behaviors? If so, what must you do to show her you are working towards regaining her trust? Is there ever a good reason to cause shame?

You must continuously make respectful deposits into your woman's heart if you have been disrespectful to her. Display actions you know she would like and appreciate. Once she sees your dedication, you will restore her trust in the relationship. Rebuilding her faith is a process. Therefore, "RESPECT" her space and show much "PATIENCE." You can express your sincerity by showing your thoughtful actions, such as kind conversations, flowers, a nice card, a nice meal, a clean house, etc.

Here is a confession for you to pray: I am a man of excellence, and I excel in all that I do. I think big, and I get big results because I serve a big God. I go the extra mile with joy to honor God and my woman. I am a man of high standards just like Joseph, and I will maintain my standards no matter the circumstances. I am an overcomer; therefore, I succeed in all that I do. Thank You, Father, for helping me with this transformation. I am a real man, and I will demonstrate this stance daily, in Jesus' name. Amen.

See if you remember what you read in this chapter.

We should picture _____ _____ _____ in everyone.

43

A Real Man Makes Good Decisions

Matthew 1:18-19 18 Now the birth of Jesus Christ took place under these circumstances: When His mother Mary had been promised in marriage to Joseph, before they came together, she was found to be pregnant {through the power} of the Holy Spirit. 19 And her {promised} husband Joseph, being a just and upright man and not willing to expose her publicly and to shame and disgrace her, **decided** to repudiate and dismiss {divorce} her quietly and secretly {Amplified Bible}.

A real man makes good decisions. You are the leader, and your leadership abilities are based on you making the right decisions at the right time. Never produce a move centered on your intellect {emotions}. Be certain that all of your movements are formed by your heart {spirit}. Joseph functioned in this manner. He mastered the art of decision making, and everyone gained from his portrait. Manufacturing good choices is an art. If people could see into your mind's drawings, would they love what they see? Are your mental sketches vibrant or dull colors? Joseph's mental artwork impressed God. As a result, God gave him the responsibility to raise Jesus.

Scroll down your mind's gallery. What has the Lord chosen for you to draw {mental images}? Are you drawing them? Scan the canvas of your brain. Are your decisions a depiction of a Picasso original or a bootleg copy? The results of your decisions paint priceless or worthless pictures. The mental picture you paint will eventually become the physical portrait you embrace. There is a war taking place daily, and the battlefield is your mind. Your victories and losses are all settled by your thoughts. Your brain is the processing center. It is the area where you separate perception from the truth. A real man is a thinker. The human mind is amazing; however, it has to be trained. You train your mind by having thinking sessions. When was the last time you meditated on your options? When was the last time you sat down and thought your way through a particular problem using a one step at a time approach?

During your thinking sessions, weigh all of your options, and throw away what goes against your heart. Your heart is like a smoke detector. It detects the fire before it actually begins. There are two keys to thinking sessions. First, write down your choices and meditate on them. Second, talk your way through your possibilities. Do not speak in your mind, but rather, speak aloud. Your brain is a muscle, and thinking sessions are a great way to strengthen it. If you do not effectively utilize thinking sessions, your life will be heavily challenged. If your mental state is out of control, nobody wins. Joseph was great at handling his reactions. It is safe to say his mind's eye was in the center of the storm and controlled it. Difficult issues are always accompanied by some sort of downpour. Bad decisions are a sign that you are bothered by the thunder. If you are in a cyclone, you need a "Time-Out." Take a pause, and grant your mind the opportunity to disconnect from the eruption. A clear mind weathers all storms.

Do you like sports? What is your favorite sport? How fast do you call for a "Time-Out" when your team is playing poorly? If you yell for a break when your team is in trouble, are you also yelling for a break when your decisions are in trouble? It is all about making the right decision at the right time when it matters the most which is always. One wise decision will place you in the winner's circle; however, a defective decision can cost you everything. The truth is your ability to make good or bad decisions is solely up to you alone.

We live in a world of countless choices. For example, we decide what to wear and what to eat every day. Some decisions are easy to make while others require lots of patience and need a critical "Time-Out." One of the most important decisions you will make is the one concerning your significant other. The right choice will result in a "marriage made in Heaven," but the wrong pick will be nothing short of the next world war.

You must master the art of decision making before making a decision. If you do not master the art of decision making, your decisions will ultimately master you. Anything you are not able to conquer will eventually conquer you. If you are not able to think like a winner, you will become a slave to your thought life.

My son was behaving poorly one day, and I wanted him to reflect on his bad choices. At that moment, God revealed His "Time-Out" principles to me along with a life changing statement. God said, "Antonio is who you once were {a child}, and you are who he will become {an adult}. If "Time-Out" is effective for him to learn and grow, "Time-Out" is good for you." This revelation was life changing.

I became the master decision maker once I began to implement constant "Time-Outs." Taking "Time-Outs" is now a daily practice of mine. It gives me the opportunity to reflect and listen to God's instructions. I have made bad choices in the past. I have the scars to prove the abuse of these choices. I lost so much. For instance, sometime ago, I developed a strong desire to own a BMW to impress everyone. Ego always chauffeurs a person off of the cliff. My wife advised me not to buy the car since I did not need it. I already had a nice car. Foolishly, I refused to listen to her advice and made a senseless investment. Six months later, I sold the car and lost money in the process. The new and improved me would never make a costly decision without taking a "Time-Out" to reflect on the pros and cons of my decision. It can take a lifetime to correct a bad choice that was based on excitement or impulsive thinking.

We live in a fast-paced world, and for this reason, we all need daily "Time-Outs." They help to avoid emotional build-ups. Think about all of the subjects you deal with during the course of a day. Consider the unresolved topics which you have stored up in you. What do you suppose happens once you run out of storage space? You explode. Men, let us be honest with ourselves, and recognize that most of us chose to internalize our problems. For some reason, we believe it is the best way to deal with issues. This choice is terrible since it results in more eruptions than an overheated volcano. How many times have you made an unhealthy ruling due to a build-up? Your choice to suppress issues will never benefit you, your woman, or children. You need to release these matters on a daily basis.

I once was ruled by my emotions; therefore, my ability to make skillful decisions was hindered. I struggled terribly with anger. This uncontrollable rage ruled my life for a very long time. I attended anger management classes several times, read numerous books, and tried meditation, but nothing I attempted worked. When I lost control, I experienced a rapid heartbeat, perspiring palms, blurred vision, and distorted hearing. It even impacted my ability to speak as my anger literally took my speech away. I know you are probably saying, "He sounds like The Incredible Hulk." To be honest, I felt like him. I did everything he did except turn green. I was constantly losing control of the steering wheel and leaving a steady trace of the smoky collisions. I had to accept the truth that my marriage and other affiliations were suffering due to my inability to master my emotions.

All the books I read and classes I attended left me frustrated and confused. Let us be honest, it is difficult to count from one hundred to one backwards once you are so frustrated that your perspective is "MIA" {missing in action}. I desperately needed help so I sought the answers from God, and He taught me how to apply the "Time-Out" principles. Prior to His life changing lessons, I had learned principles on controlling my emotions. The lessons He taught me clarified this key point that I did not need to control my emotions as much as I needed to "master" my emotions. Similar to a car which suddenly malfunctions, you can have control of its steering wheel and in an instant lose control. However, once you master your emotions, the vehicle is always in your orderly possession – responsibility.

Have you ever stated or heard someone say, "I do not know what happened, but I just blacked out and lost control?" For this reason, you must become the ruler of your emotions. There is a greater level of responsibility once you decide to master your responses. When you are the owner of your actions, you let go of excuses. If you are able to distinguish between good and bad, you are able to master your emotions and masterly make the right decisions. You must take ownership of your actions. You take possession of them by holding yourself accountable.

God gave me a challenge one day. He instructed me to eliminate the word "BUT." I accepted His challenge and quickly learned that eliminating the word "but" was not going to be easy, although it was very necessary. How often do you utilize the word "but" when you are justifying your actions? I applied that word frequently. "I did this, "but" she did that. "But," you do not know what she said to me." This blaming conversation is the source of the problem. You must get your "but" out of the way. The word "but" is often used when you are attempting to strengthen your excuses. An example often seen is someone caught speeding and responds, "but" I was not the only one." Do you see why this word should be deleted from your vocabulary at certain times?

49

When I began to utilize "Time-Out," I literally sat in a corner, faced the wall, and reflected on my actions and choices. By doing so, I learned how to master my emotions which helped me to become a master decision maker. My wife no longer calls me, "The Incredible Hulk or Dr. Jekyll and Mr. Hyde," now she calls me, "The love of her life, her best friend, and her everything." I thank the Lord for teaching me the "Time-Out" principles. My wife really loves my calm demeanor and ability to think like a winner. A real man sits in a corner, faces the wall, and reflects. Your willingness to reflect carefully will improve your relationship with God, your woman, and children.

Joseph's ability to effectively communicate to himself was a key source of his outcome. A real man is the master of effective communication by speaking to himself before he speaks to anyone else. Lots of men are not good at conversing with their woman because they are not good at conversing with themselves. We have been taught not to speak much and to keep our feelings bottled up. I once functioned in this fashion until I realized that my ability to make clever decisions and to communicate effectively goes hand in hand. Making skilled decisions requires skillful interaction. If nothing else, you have to skillfully navigate your way through life by self-talk. I believe Joseph's self-talk practice was one of his greatest weapons which profited everyone involved, and it secured God's plan. Consider the truth that everyone is not going to always listen to you, but you are always listening to yourself.

If you are not able to successfully speak to yourself, you will not be able to successfully speak to others. Self-talk is critical. It helps you to reflect on all of your options. More often than not, people are great at talking their way into trouble and do a lousy job at talking their way out of trouble. Think about the times when a well needed self-talk session would have benefitted you. Contemplate on the gains you could have accomplished if you had skillfully talked your way through an issue. Consider the wasted time and unnecessary hurts and pains which you encountered because you did not skillfully speak to yourself. Was it worth it? A skillful communicator understands the power of words and utilizes them effectively. You are going to accomplish more out of life when your discussions are attached with honor rather than dishonor.

The "Time-Out" way of life exists for this reason. Once the coach of your team calls for a "Time-Out," he is giving the players sound advice and strategies to win the game. While you are in "Time-Out," you should give yourself sound advice and winning strategies so you can win at the game of life. "Time-Out" is simply a way to keep your emotions in check and regroup. If your peace is absent, you cannot make trustworthy judgments or communicate effectively.

Become proactive to avoid eruptions. The result of a flare-up is very harmful to you, your woman, and children. Have enough discipline to sit in a corner and face the wall as much as you need. Unlike your sports team, you do not have a limited amount of "Time-Outs." Therefore, take as many "Time-Outs" as needed to make winning plays for your team. Your teammates {woman and children} will really appreciate your heartfelt communication. No one feels secure in a relationship where impulsive decisions are being made. You are the leader of your family. God designed marriages to function in this manner. I said, "Leader," not dictator. Remember, your decisions must value everyone.

A second point of view pertaining to the word "decided" is that a real man does not waiver in his decisions. Your partner will not feel secure if you are not able to make a decision and stick to it. Women desire stability. Like a ship in the midst of a rocky sea so is a man who waivers with his philosophy. "If any of you lacks

51

wisdom, he should ask God, who gives generously to all without finding fault, and it will be given to him. But when he asks, he must believe and not doubt, because he who doubts is like a wave of the sea, blown and tossed by the wind. That man should not think he will receive anything from the Lord; he is a double-minded man, unstable in all he does." {James 1:5-8NIV}.

A double-minded man is like a roller coaster ride. He is up one minute and down the next. I once operated in this fashion, and it was damaging for me and my marriage. My wife and I had many fights and disagreements over me being double-minded. She never felt comfortable with my decisions. How could she? I did not feel comfortable with them as shown by the constant changing of my mind. Talk about an inner battle. How can you trust a man to lead his family if he is not able to make decisions and stick to them?

Flip/flopping with your views is like living on a question mark {?}, and this lukewarm way of living represents shaky grounds. Who wants to live on a question mark? A real man does not stand on wavering thoughts since he is secure with his beliefs. Would you share these thoughts with your woman, "I have made the decision, and I am not sure this outcome will work, but let us hope this choice is the right one for us?" Does this conversation even sound right? It is your responsibility to gather all of the required information even if it commands extensive research. Accepting this role demonstrates leadership and security. Remember, it is your job to cover your woman and not expose her to any unnecessary stress. Leadership and protection is what a real man looks like and does.

A real man lives on a period {.}. A period represents sturdy grounds. The following statement is how a real man addresses his woman. "I have made the decision, and I am very comfortable with knowing that we are going to benefit from it." Do you see the difference? You are the leader. If you are wavering with your decisions, everyone involved will be wavering as well. I have to admit that it can be difficult to make decisions at times. How many times have you asked yourself this question, "How do I know if I am making the right choice?" As you struggle, remember to enter "Time-Out" and have a conversation with God.

All of your decisions should be founded on the wisdom of God. God's wisdom is His word. I encourage you to open your Bible and search for the answers which you need. It is the book of countless replies to all of life's questions. "Wisdom is the principal thing; therefore get wisdom: and with all thy getting get understanding" {Proverbs 4:7KJV}. You will never have a problem that cannot be solved or answered because God has supplied us with the book of good judgment. Reading the Bible replaces the shaky grounds {?} with sturdy grounds {.}.

The Creator never fails. He has the remedy for all discomforts. It is great to have His plans as a means of living. He has given you completely what you need in His word. Pressures are removed once you seek the Scriptures for answers. We should not fail at life since the keys are given to us in the Bible. God has granted every one of us an open book test. All we have to do is open the Bible, study, and apply its contents. These are the essential ingredients to making the right decisions.

The confidence that you are going to display to your woman will protect her more than you know. Words cannot explain what this firm belief will do for you both and the children. These principles which you are learning must be applied daily in order for you to obtain the changes that you are seeking. It is a proven system; however, it must be worked, and worked, and worked. Consistency is the key word here.

I am not describing a transformation that could possibly happen. I am describing a transformation that will definitely happen if you sincerely want it. It worked for Joseph, and it continues to work for me as well. I pray you have the passion, dedication, focus, and remain consistent throughout this journey. Remember, anything worth having requires all of you. Press on my friend, "THE BEST IS YET TO COME."

Ladies, express what your needs are to your man. When you take the guessing game out of the equation, he will function better. Do not leave it up to him to figure out what you mean, but tell him exactly what you mean. Make it as simple as black and white. By doing so, you will eliminate any gray area. Remember, gray areas symbolize uncertainty {?} which will result in confusion. It is better for you both if he invests his time in making good decisions instead of trying to crack a code. You two are a team, and teamwork is very important for the success of your journey. Set aside daily "Time-Outs" with him, and share your sincere feelings about everything. Also, utilize these moments to share your needs with each other. Hold nothing back. As he helps you, he is also helping himself.

As men, our minds are constantly racing and thinking about the next move toward success. For this reason, I would like for you to view yourself as your man's coach. Reinforce the "Time-Out" principles and the importance of them. View effective communication as the glue that holds your family together.

Listen attentively to your man during these quiet periods of communication, and you will learn about his fears, frustrations, and any hindrances. At that point, begin to coach him through the problems by utilizing the Word of God. My wife coached me by using the Scriptures, and those sessions played a major role in my transformation. Those settings brought us closer together and reinforced our partnership and union. During our sessions, I felt confident since I had a person fighting for me.

It is much easier for your man to accomplish his goals when you both are working together as a team. The Lord loves unity. It is a principle which He supports. Therefore, you both need to understand the power of mutual agreement as this practice is extremely important. "Again, I tell you that if two of you on earth agree about anything you ask for, it will be done for you by my Father in heaven. For where two or three come together in my name, there I am with them" {Matthew 18:19-20NIV}.

I am not suggesting that you become so consumed in your man to the point of neglecting yourself. Your actions and support are evidence to the truth that you are with him every step of the way. You are his helper as Eve was Adam's helper. With this point understood, he needs to take this journey with your support but without a dependence on you. You cannot transform him. He needs to transform for himself. Ultimately, his transformation is contingent upon his determination and desires, not your determination and desires.

If you feel overwhelmed at some point, back up and let God take control. Remember, He is the only one who can truly help your man with his transformation. Your coaching has to come from the Lord in order to experience real success. He will let you know what to do and how to do it. You must have balance. The Creator is the one who will give you both the necessary stability as you move forward to having a deep relationship based on His instructions.

Here is a prayer for you: Father, thank You for "Deshawn's" ability to make good decisions. "Deshawn" is not double-minded. "Deshawn" skillfully makes his decisions based on Your word. Thank You for filling him with Your wisdom. Thank You for showing him how to select the options that benefits our family. Help me with my decisions as well. Teach me how to communicate effectively with "Deshawn" so I may assist him in the decision making process. Father, give us both the necessary stability we need. I am grateful that we are both working as a team. We are thinking like winners, and we are experiencing success as a family, in Jesus' name. Amen.

Reflection

Please take the time to journal your questions and comments as a powerful way to track your progress. These moments are when you take the time to reflect on what you have learned in this chapter and express your thoughts. What did you learn from this chapter? Are you the type of man who waivers with his decisions? If so, why are you not confident with your decisions? Did the introduction of the "Time-Out" principle help you? How many "Time-Outs" should you take during the course of a day? How are you going to prove to your woman you can make good decisions and be an effective communicator? What is your guide from this day forward while making decisions? How important is it for you to wait until the answer is revealed? What is the best way to avoid an eruption?

Practice communicating with your woman for at least thirty minutes at the end of each day, and attentively listen to what she has to say. The key word here is "listen." While you are listening to her, you are demonstrating love and respect. A real man cares for all of the needs of his woman. There is nothing too big or too small because if it matters to her, it should matter to you. Embracing this approach will work wonders for your relationship. Just as a man needs respect, a woman needs security. Prove to her you are on the right path by effectively communicating with her. By doing so, she will acknowledge you as "The Master of Decision Making."

There is a man on death row at this very moment because he refused to sit in a corner and face the wall when that option was freely available. Now, he is forced to take daily "Time-Outs" as he waits for the day of his execution.

Here is a confession for you to pray: I am a man of excellence, and I excel in all that I do. I think big, and I get big results because I serve a big God. I go the extra mile with joy to honor God and my woman. I am a man of high standards just like Joseph, and I will maintain my standards no matter the circumstances. I am an overcomer; therefore, I succeed in all that I do. Thank You, Father, for helping me with this transformation. I am a real man, and I will demonstrate this stance daily, in Jesus' name. Amen.

See if you remember what you read in this chapter.

What is the best way to avoid a build up? What is a great way to relieve stress?

____ ____ ____ ____ ____ ____ ____.

A Real Man Understands the Strength in Quietness

Matthew 1:18-19 18 Now the birth of Jesus Christ took place under these circumstances: When His mother Mary had been promised in marriage to Joseph, before they came together, she was found to be pregnant {through the power} of the Holy Spirit. 19 And her {promised} husband Joseph, being a just and upright man and not willing to expose her publicly and to shame and disgrace her, decided to repudiate and dismiss {divorce} her **quietly** and secretly {Amplified Bible}.

A real man understands the power of quietness as Joseph did. His ability to deal with his challenges quietly displayed amazing control and inner strength. Remember, a real man processes circumstances internally and not externally. Internally is the place where quietness rules, and externally is the place where chaos rules. When Joseph decided to deal with Mary quietly, he clearly heard the voice of God which muzzled the mouth of the enemy.

The Lord is always speaking, but we are not always listening. Before He created this planet and everything in it, He spoke about it first {Read Genesis Chapter 1}. The Creator rules the Heavens and earth by His words. He is "The" Great Communicator, and there is not another like Him. Hearing His instructions is of great importance; however, many of us are missing His valuable commands since our mind is not clear. The number one assignment of chaos is to weaken the voice of God and to strengthen the voice of the enemy.

A real man demonstrates quietness in more ways than one. There are two forms of quietness you have to display in order to please God and your woman. The first form is the obvious one. Keep your mouth shut. This acceptance is essential regarding effective communication. "You both can sing together, but you both cannot talk together." Your woman needs to be heard, and once she is able to freely express herself, it proves to her how important she is to you. Your silence speaks to her heart by saying, "I respect your feelings and thoughts. I am concerned about what you have to say. You have the freedom to express yourself." Remember, she needs security, and your silence is a great way to display security. If my wife is speaking, I remain silent. The reason is I am processing everything she is saying. I am listening for concerns that are obvious and for concerns that are not so obvious. A real man becomes a private investigator by listening carefully to his woman as she speaks. It is great to listen to her conversations but even better to listen to her heart.

Your silence does not reveal weakness. Rather, it is proof of your inner strength, discipline, and character. Have you ever heard the saying, "Loose lips sink ships?" How many ships have you sunk because you were not willing to mute yourself? When a man is arrested he is given "the right to remain silent." Why? Anything he says can and will be used against him in the court of law. And still, people incriminate themselves every day by speaking. Amazing! When a judge calls for "order in the court," he is demanding for everyone to be quiet so he can regain control of the courtroom. Order and control are present when silence is displayed at the right time.

Your silence protects, removes any and all strife, and eases tensions. God desires to be the mediator in your conversations. Once He is allowed to mediate, He will reveal the truth to you or your lady concerning any issues. All battles are not worth fighting, and some battles are won when a person says nothing at all. My mouth was often my worst enemy, and as a result, my wife and I had senseless fights and did not speak to each other for days. I was too busy wanting to be right and in control. If I would have remained silent at the right time, the days of separation, battles, and the lonely feelings I experienced would not have occurred. I have realized that it is more important for me to have peace in my marriage instead of constant conflict. Therefore, I settle certain issues by placing a muzzle on my mouth.

Silence is a disciplined practice, especially if you are angry. I hurt my wife in many ways due to the harmful words I once utilized out of anger. I am proud to say that my toxic remarks are a thing of the past, and we are now closer than ever. My choice to remain silent has been helpful in the rebuilding process. God's voice is the leading voice in our relationship. Therefore, the voice of pride is not an issue. "Silence is golden." The Bible says that there is, "A time to be quiet and a time to speak" {Ecclesiastes 3:7NLT}.

You must be skillful in order to display the second type of quietness. A real man understands that his whisper is more powerful than his yell. He does not speak in a loud voice to intimidate his woman, and he is always mindful of his tone. Often, it is not what you say that can be harmful, but the damage is in how you say it. Words are powerful, "Death and life are in the power of the tongue, and they who indulge in it shall eat the fruit of it {for death or life}" {Proverbs 18:21AMP}. Words are alive. Words transport positive or negative energy. Therefore, you must deliver your words properly along with the proper tone. God says, "A man has joy in making an apt answer, and a word spoken at the right moment—how good it is" {Proverbs 15:23AMP}.

I believe Joseph spoke to Mary while they were dealing with the issue of her unexpected pregnancy. Joseph displayed self-control throughout this entire story. For this reason, I believe his conversations were attached with love. Gentleness to this degree means, you speak to be understood more than to be heard. When your words are kind, they reflect soundless confidence.

Quietness is an attitude of peace in the face of adversity. A real man controls the atmosphere by the tone of his remarks. Obstacles do not control you, but you maneuver the barriers. You exhibit self-control to your woman by simply using the right words along with the right pitch. How would you feel if you saw your favorite singer perform and his or her performance was out of pitch? Would that be music to your ears? When your sound is loud, disrespectful, harmful, and egotistic, is it pleasing to your woman's hearing? My wife recently told me, "I enjoy being around you because it just feels good." Pleasant vibrations sway people and animals. You can even charm a poisonous snake with the right melody. Bad communication shatters relationships, but a good exchange glues them together.

Think about how your woman feels when you exhibit voice control. View your vocal cords as the strings of a well-played guitar. Imagine how enjoyable your days will become once you regularly hit the right note. Consider the applauses that she is going to give you for your outstanding musical. Let your words and tones entertain her as "music to her ears." I desire for my voice to be my wife's favorite melody; therefore, I work on my pitch continuously. Success is not achieved in a fitting moment, but it is reached by a tailored lifestyle. The more I practice my tone of voice, the simpler it is for me to converse in this mode. Speaking quietly requires constant practice. The more you exercise these principles, the easier it will be for you to demonstrate them. I compare the constant rehearsal to breathing. You do not think about breathing, you "Just do it." Your ability to lead requires skills, and lots of work is needed in order for you to obtain them. "If the ax is dull and its edge unsharpened, more strength is needed but skill will bring success" {Ecclesiastes 10:10NIV}.

A real man understands that peaceful times outweighs periods of war. I do all I can to be in the best standings with my wife. This attempt does not mean we do not have disagreements because we do. However, we skillfully solve all of our differences by the standards I am sharing with you. I am in charge of keeping the right atmosphere in my marriage, and I secure this ambiance by displaying either form of quietness. I do not allow myself to engage in an angry quarrel. Who can quarrel by themselves? When my wife and I argued in the past, I wanted her to shut her mouth. I told her, "Why don't you just shut up?" I had so much to learn. First of all, I have no power over her or what she chooses to say. After all, it is her mouth. Secondly, I wanted her to shut up, and yet, I kept speaking. I am thrilled that I am able to look back and reflect on the mess I once had in my marriage. I had no control over myself, but I wanted to have control over her. A real sign of control would have been for me to shut my mouth. I have decided that my wife is too valuable, and I will not waste time displaying anything other than love towards her. I remain silent if she begins to argue, and she eventually stops. We solve all interferences in a principled manner. Here is my whisper, "Honey, you are too valuable to me, and I refuse to fight with you. I love you." Those magical words along with the proper tone are my approach towards her which melts her anger just like butter. Try this approach the next time you and your woman begin to argue.

Ladies, many of you have a problem remaining silent. I recognize that this response is a way of defending yourself. Another attitude to consider is to let your silence guide your man to the truth. This reaction defends you more than you can imagine. Once my wife took this stance, it made me think about the foolishness I was creating. By seeing her poise, I accepted responsibility for my actions. Her composure showed me there was no way of escape. It kept the focus on me, and I was not able to shift the attention to her.

At one time, I attempted to entice my wife to speak for the purpose of twisting things around and shifting the negative energy. I can remember her saying to me, "I can't believe how you twisted this whole thing around. How did this issue become about me?" Like a police officer who is arresting a criminal, anything she said I used against her. As soon as she learned what I was doing and changed her approach, I was left to deal with the truth, the whole truth, and nothing but the truth. You need to be in partnership with the Lord. He will let you know when to speak and when not to speak. He will also let you know what to say and when to say it. I believe certain differences are not worth discussing. Know the difference between what is important and what is not important. This knowledge is a great key to possess. It locks the doors to unhealthy discussions and attitudes. Your self-control is strength. Your appropriate words used at the suitable time with a positive tone are strengths as well.

Here is a prayer for you: Father, teach me when to remain silent and when to speak. Allow my peace to speak even when I am not speaking. Show me how to use the right words at the right time and how to deliver them. I desire to communicate with "Peter" in a respectful and effective way. Also, impart to "Peter" the importance of utilizing the appropriate tone along with the proper words. Give "Peter" an attentive ear for my concerns. Make the truth be known to him that his quietness displays strength and not weakness. I am grateful that "Peter" is not prideful. I am appreciative for his humility and his concern regarding the nurturing of our union and family. I thank You in advance for answering this prayer, in Jesus' name. Amen.

Reflection

Please take the time to journal your questions and comments as a powerful way to track your progress. These moments are when you take the time to reflect on what you have learned in this chapter and express your thoughts. What did you learn from this chapter? How are you going to display quietness to your woman? Are you struggling with this concept, and if so, why? Do you always have to have the last word? Are your thoughts and ideas better than your woman's thoughts and ideas? Does the concept of remaining silent challenge your manhood? How are you going to train your tone? Whose voice should be the leading voice in your relationship {yours, your woman's, or God's}?

Here is a confession for you to pray: I am a man of excellence, and I excel in all that I do. I think big, and I get big results because I serve a big God. I go the extra mile with joy to honor God and my woman. I am a man of high standards just like Joseph, and I will maintain my standards no matter the circumstances. I am an overcomer; therefore, I succeed in all that I do. Thank You, Father, for helping me with this transformation. I am a real man, and I will demonstrate this stance daily, in Jesus' name. Amen.

See if you remember what you read in this chapter.

Your silence demonstrates

____ ____ ____ ____ ____ ____ ____ ____.

A Real Man Keeps a Secret

Matthew 1:18-19 18 Now the birth of Jesus Christ took place under these circumstances: When His mother Mary had been promised in marriage to Joseph, before they came together, she was found to be pregnant {through the power} of the Holy Spirit. 19 And her {promised} husband Joseph, being a just and upright man and not willing to expose her publicly and to shame and disgrace her, decided to repudiate and dismiss {divorce} her quietly and **secretly** {Amplified Bible}.

Since a real man is trustworthy, he can keep a secret. Joseph did not deal with Mary openly. He chose to deal with her secretly. He knew exposing her publicly would have only made matters worse. Keeping this issue undisclosed was his way of protecting her. Joseph's amazing character was truly on display during this challenging time. It is very difficult to be confidential, especially if you feel you were deceived as Joseph must have felt. Keeping this situation private had to have been quite a challenge for him, and yet, he held onto his principles.

If your woman shares a secret with you, keep it to yourself. Her decision to open up is her way of saying, "I have faith in you," and you do not want to tamper with her trust. There are private matters that she will only express to you because of the degree of intimacy you both have with each other. These secrets should never be repeated to anyone else. If she discovers that you have disclosed her conversations with others, the faith she has in you will be destroyed. Her secrets provide you with another time to remain silent.

Joseph put his feelings aside in order to protect Mary's feelings. He was more concerned with her image than his own. Can you imagine the price he paid to take this stance? All of the facts of this story indicated to Joseph that Mary had committed adultery, and still, Joseph chose to protect her by not saying a word. Is it not amazing how the facts that we know can change, but the truth never changes because it always remains the same? His actions spoke loudly and clearly. Keeping the circumstances a secret said, "I will deal with the hurt and pain so you {Mary} will not have to deal with the hurt and pain." A real man is concerned with the well-being of his woman in spite of the situation. Have you ever told a secret that your lady had entrusted to you? How did you feel once you shared it? Was there any feeling of uneasiness, guilt, or shame?

For the most part, people deal with the issues in their relationship too openly. Freely sharing your household business is inappropriate since it opens the door to outside voices and opinions. The influences and attitudes of others have the ability to control how we feel and respond to circumstances. Think about how many divorces are carried out in the public. Think about how these people are influenced by what others say about them. Think about how they try to defend themselves to the public and then become bitter with their mate. How can people say, "I do" out of love and yet display so much hate when they are going through a separation or a divorce? Does love respond in this fashion? Of course not! Love never fails, love never changes, and love remains the same.

My admiration for Joseph grew even more due to his position of secrecy. Joseph's silence ensured damage control. His quietness contained the circumstances. If he had shared the secret, it would have inflamed the situation. Revealing a private matter is unwise since it makes the condition uncontainable. Is it easier to contain a spark or a raging inferno? A real man does not participate in gossip. "Avoid godless chatter, because those who indulge in it will become more and more ungodly. Their teaching will spread like gangrene" {2ⁿᵈ Timothy 2:16-17NIV}.

Since a real man does not embrace scandal, he is admired and respected by others. When he is present, rumors are absent. His position of integrity is known and valued. Gossipers and thieves share the commonality of both causing damage and destruction whenever they are around. Godless chatter slanders a person's name, it adds its own details to a particular story, and it hurts people. Gossip is like poison creating more internal damage than external harm. Gossiping is not what a real man does. A real man is comfortable with speaking directly to a person instead of talking behind his or her back. Joseph was man of integrity, a man of truth, and his ethics outweighed the circumstances he faced.

A real man is reliable. Joseph demonstrated honor when he chose not to share Mary's pregnancy. Honor is consistent behavior whether behind closed doors or out in the open. Many of us are walking around daily with two different faces. We put on make-up perfectly for the public, but they never get to see the real person behind the foundation. Honor is one of the most important characteristics that a person should possess. Joseph did not forget the dedication he had for Mary. He did not want the hurt and pain that he was dealing with to spread any further. A real man's appearance always displays just and upright actions. Joseph was a man among men who showed us how to live an honorable life. A man with goodness to this degree will always be rewarded by God. Joseph was rewarded by being selected as the father of Jesus.

My own mother never involved herself with gossip, and she is the model I imitate. I remember her always saying, "If you cannot say it to a person's face, do not say it behind their back." My wife tells me how much she admires the fact that I do not indulge in hearsay. She knows if she tells me something, it will not go any further.

I am passionate about the importance of maintaining a secret. I have experienced betrayal when a person shared a sidebar conversation that I had with them. At that moment, I felt vulnerable and embarrassed. Trust is not something you can build overnight, and it is not easily reestablished once a person is betrayed. Never share any heart-to-heart conversations your woman has with you, unless it is life threatening or could result in danger to her or others. Never use any of her secrets as a means of hurting her, especially if you two are having an argument. For example, the comment, "That is why you were abused as a child," would be terribly damaging. If her secret is that she was verbally or physically abused as a child and you repeat this cruelty in an argument with her, you are not allowing her to heal and move on in life.

As her protector, you are similar to a safe deposit box, where she deposits important documents {secrets}. It is your job to make her feel secure at all times. You must lock up the records and not tamper with them unless she chooses to retrieve them from you. Viewing yourself as her safe deposit box is very powerful. Your support helps her deal with troubling matters and establishes deep trust with you.

Mary was carrying a baby who presented an initial problem for Joseph, and your woman may also be carrying something which presents to be a problem. If this situation pertains to you, follow Joseph's examples. Express attentiveness and sensitivity to whatever the concern may be. Do not begin to judge and criticize her or focus on your feelings. Joseph did not judge and criticize Mary or focus on his feelings and neither should you. Consider that all relationships are tested at some point, and only the strong at heart {amazing faith} survive.

Lots of men have deserted a valuable woman believing her circumstances were impossible to solve. Joseph shows us we can get to the bottom of all circumstances once the Creator is in the center of the union. Confronting and hurdling obstacles as a team helps your connection to grow stronger and better. Sometimes, secrets are painful, embarrassing, and can torment a person. These feelings infiltrate every part of a person's life, and your family unit will be impacted by the negative energy. You must help your lady overcome any anxieties by assisting her to regain her liberation. Like a boxer, stand toe to toe with her and knockout that meddling opponent. She will never overcome the secret if she does not fight for her deliverance. Covering up the secret or running from it is not the answer.

Have you ever been in the delivery room as your woman gave birth to your child? Did you hold her hands and encourage her with ever push? How did you feel once the baby was born? Words cannot express the experience of giving birth. You must be there for your lady, hold her hands, encourage, and coach her every step of the way. God has designed for you to help with the delivery of your child just as God wants you to aid your woman when she is facing difficult problems. You must encourage your woman to move forward. Secrets hold you in the past, but as you support her, she will overcome the turmoil and be free.

The Lord is so amazing! He functions at times in ways we do not always understand, yet, whatever He does always works out for our good. "For My thoughts are not your thoughts, neither are your ways My ways, says the Lord. For as the heavens are higher than the earth, so are My ways higher than your ways and My thoughts than your thoughts" {Isaiah 55:8-9AMP}. "And we know that God causes everything to work together for the good of those who love God and are called according to his purpose for them" {Romans 8:28NLT}.

God did not create any bad situations that have occurred to your woman. However, He will utilize these events to strengthen her in every area of her life. I have learned that God utilizes the worst circumstances to bring out the very best in us. Look at the life of Joseph and Mary. They were faced with many obstacles, and yet, Jesus was the result of their teamwork. The Father utilized a condition that seemed hopeless and gave us all hope in the form of Jesus. You can triumph over any obstacle once the Creator is your advisor. Jesus said, "With man this is impossible, but with God all things are possible" {Matthew 19:26NIV}.

Try using these steps to help your woman overcome an irritating secret:

1.   Ask her if there is anything bothering her because you want to help with any issues she has.

2.   Stand in unity and fight for her liberation. Since there is power in numbers, convey to her that there is nothing you two cannot conquer together. "How could one person chase a thousand of them, and two people put ten thousand to flight?" {Deuteronomy 32:30NLT}.

3.   Tell her you are available in any capacity that she needs.

4.   Deal with the difficulty one bite at a time. It is easier to eat an elephant piece by piece instead of attempting to eat it whole.

5.   Seek the Lord for the solution. Answers are obtained by praying, reading the Bible, and relying on God to guide you.

6.   Do not make the matter bigger than the Creator. What you magnify grows; therefore, amplify the key and not the lock.

7.   Be very patient with her. Shower her with lots of support as though she was covered in layers of soap. Let your attitude reflect your concern and sensitivity.

8.   Tell her she is the most important person in the world to you. Let her know that your love for her will only increase as you both triumph over the secret together. Pray with her constantly to reassure her that the answer is in God, and that He will help you both to overcome the secret.

Your loving attention will eventually pay off so look forward to it.   Like the Fourth of July, she will have her day of independence.   Therefore, I am celebrating with you in advance. Praise the Lord! You both made it through a challenging time and are experiencing a lovely relationship. These are the secrets of the second greatest love story ever written.   The first greatest love story ever written is God's love for us through Jesus.   Be encouraged!

Ladies, gossip is a terrible practice. I recommend you do not indulge in it at all. If your man shares a secret with you, do not share it with anyone else. However, if your life is threatened, if you are experiencing any type of abuse, or if there is potential harm that may occur to you, your man, or anyone else, share the secret immediately.   Again, it is all about freedom.   Do not compromise your freedom or safety because you feel obligated not to tell. Because of your courage to notify someone, he will no longer be imprisoned by the secret. Use wise judgment.   Never sacrifice doing the right thing for a false sense of loyalty. You should never be loyal to danger. As his woman, you are his helper. Your honesty is another way of helping him become a real man.

I admire my wife's perspective because she kept our challenging circumstances to herself. Like a blanket, she covered me. I looked pleasant to others even though my actions were unpleasant. My wife did not gossip with her family and friends; however, she did talk with the Lord and used Him as her outlet. God knows how to keep a secret, and He will share a secret for the betterment of the bigger picture. King David secretly committed adultery and murder. The Creator shared these sins with the Prophet Nathan. When Nathan addressed David about his evil actions, it helped David to confess his sins. The confession restored the connection that David had with the Creator {Read 2nd Samuel Chapter 12}.

I believe in seeking all solutions from God. He sees and knows everything. He helped me with a secret that I was holding back from my wife by giving me the courage to tell her. I did not want to hurt her, but the secret was causing us more harm than good. Sometimes, we have to take big steps in order to correct our path. The huge stride I took in sharing this painful secret was definitely a step in the right direction. It strongly reinforced our relationship. It is amazing what the truth does for us when we decide to embrace it. God does not want us in bondage. "I will say to the prisoners, 'Come out in freedom,' and to those in darkness, 'Come into the light" {Isaiah 49:9NLT}.

If you are holding onto a troubling matter and do not know how to share it with your man, simply seek God. He will give you the confidence and courage to share whatever is bothering you. Nothing should come between you and your man. If he truly cares for you, he will understand and love you through it all. My wife also had some secrets and when she shared them with me, my love for her did not change one bit. Actually, I am falling deeper and deeper in love with her by the day. A family is strengthened by their ability to jump over the stumbling blocks.

Troubling secrets robs you of your confidence and can lead to the development of paranoia. Paranoia adds unwanted stress to your relationship and life. Life is to be enjoyed so enjoy it. Do not let anything or anyone stop you from laughing hard, smiling widely, and loving more. Have you ever heard the saying, "Tell the truth, and shame the devil?" This statement is powerful. Telling the truth removes the shame from you and returns it to the one who handed it to you in the first place – the devil. He wants you to keep your mouth shut and hold you in bondage, but do not let him. Give the embarrassment back to the devil, and declare your independence today by ridding yourself of any hindering secret. Jesus came to set the captives free. "The Spirit of the Lord is on me, because he has anointed me to preach good news to the poor. He has sent me to proclaim freedom for the prisoners and recovery of sight for the blind, to release the oppressed, to proclaim the year of the Lord's favor" {Luke 4:18-19NIV}.

To the natural eye, the relationship of Joseph and Mary appeared to be dead because of their secret. You may feel as if your relationship is dead because of a secret; however, the Lord has the ability to resurrect a lifeless situation. Here is another case when the Creator revived a condition that seemed to be unresponsive. "And she went to the house of Zachariah and, entering it, saluted Elizabeth. And it occurred that when Elizabeth heard Mary's greeting, the baby leaped in her womb, and Elizabeth was filled with and controlled by the Holy Spirit. And she cried out with a loud cry, and then exclaimed, blessed {favored of God} above all other women are you! And blessed {favored of God} is the Fruit of your womb! And how {have I deserved that this honor should} be granted to me, that the mother of my Lord should come to me? For behold, the instant the sound of your salutation reached my ears, the baby in my womb leaped for joy" {Luke 1:40-44AMP}.

The baby in Elizabeth's womb leaped for joy when Mary saluted her. I believe the word joy is very important in this story. Elizabeth thought her baby was dead since she had never felt him move. Why did Mary's salutation have this type of impact on Elizabeth and the baby? Mary was also pregnant carrying God in the form of Jesus. Therefore, the presence of God generated life to the baby who appeared to be lifeless. If the Lord produced life, joy, and excitement in the womb of Elizabeth, He can produce life, joy, and excitement in your relationship. However, you have to remain in His presence. Once you pray and submit to His plan, the Lord has an entry point to all matters concerning you.

Here is a prayer for you: Father, provide "Daniel" and I with the courage to free ourselves from any hindering secrets. Give us the confidence to share with each other and not judge one another. Utilize this opportunity to knit us closer together. Use these stumbling blocks for our good. Thanks for helping and strengthening us throughout the process, in Jesus' name. Amen.

Reflection

Please take the time to journal your questions and comments as a powerful way to track your progress. These moments are when you take the time to reflect on what you have learned in this chapter and express your thoughts. What did you learn from this chapter? Are you able to keep a secret? Is integrity a big deal to you? Have you been rewarded for keeping a secret, and if so, how? What loss have you experienced because you were not able to keep a conversation private? Have you ever been betrayed by someone who shared your private discussion, and if so, how did you feel? If there is a secret haunting your woman, how are you going to help her?

Let me commend you for loving your woman enough to help her through a tough moment. Trust God during this process, and you both will end up on the right side of the matter. You can do it. Refuse to lose, and give it all you got. Think about how rewarding it is going to be when she is no longer a prisoner of the painful secret.

Here is a confession for you to pray: I am a man of excellence, and I excel in all that I do. I think big, and I get big results because I serve a big God. I go the extra mile with joy to honor God and my woman. I am a man of high standards just like Joseph, and I will maintain my standards no matter the circumstances. I am an overcomer; therefore, I succeed in all that I do. Thank You, Father, for helping me with this transformation. I am a real man, and I will demonstrate this stance daily, in Jesus' name. Amen.

See if you remember what you read in this chapter. The Bible tells us gossip spreads. What does gossip spread like?

_____ _____ _____ _____ _____ _____ _____ _____.

A Real Man Is a Thinker

Matthew 1:20 But as he was **thinking this over**, behold, an angel of the Lord appeared to him in a dream, saying, Joseph, descendant of David, do not be afraid to take Mary {as} your wife, for that which is conceived in her is of {from, out of} the Holy Spirit {Amplified Bible}.

Thinking is not an act that you perform every now and then. Thinking is an action that you do all of the time. Once you are alive, you will never have a break from your thought life. The Scripture tells us that Joseph was "thinking this over" and that "an angel of the Lord appeared to him in a dream." Amazing! Even while we are asleep, the power of reasoning is always at work. That is why you must master your thought life.

A real man is a thinker. Was Joseph pondering over the problems or was he thinking about the solution? I believe Joseph's thoughts were focused on the solution. Mary could have had a death sentence hanging over her based on the law of that time. Joseph was not comfortable with the law. Therefore, his meditations were driven by thoughtfulness. The evidence of this truth is in the story, "he was thinking this over." Doing the right thing requires thoughtful consideration while doing the wrong thing requires no thought at all. Joseph could have taken the easy route by exposing Mary and had her stoned to death. Joseph displayed the attractive features of a thinking man since he refused to take the expected traveled road. Who will not find the qualities of a problem solver appealing? Do you focus on the answers or do you focus on the problems?

Joseph was quite a thinker. Can you honestly solve problems if you are not making sensible judgments? Issues are a part of life, and there is nothing you can do to escape this reality.

Overcoming obstacles is a prerequisite for success. You will never experience any form of real success without overcoming some sort of adversity. The people who are the most successful are thinkers. A thinker does not just respond but rather thoughtfully steers his way through problems. He is cautious as he carefully approaches all matters. He is not cautious due to fear but due to processing all of the information. When you are faced with issues, do you take the time to gather and process the necessary information or do you quickly come to conclusions?

You can slap a level headed man on his cheek, and he will give you his other cheek. "If someone slaps you on one cheek, offer the other cheek also" {Luke 6:29NLT}. Profound! A focused man is not easily offended. He does not wallow in an offence. He is too busy thinking past the offence. Can you reflect wisely if you are wallowing in a hurtful experience? Notice, Joseph was "thinking." He did not quickly respond or react. He wisely thought his way through his mental maze. Many of us react too quickly and are not responding correctly to life's issues. I have made lots of mistakes in my life. Many of these mistakes could have been avoided if I had followed Joseph's standards. I should have spent my time magnifying the solutions instead of the hurtful experiences. A thinking man releases his past, for the sake of dealing with his present, and for the purpose of bettering his future.

A thinking man views problems differently than most people because he forecasts everything. This approach is a great way to weather the storms of life. He does not paint a picture based on what is seen by his natural eyes, but he paints a picture centered on what is seen by his spiritual eyes. He is not influenced by his senses but by his spirit. Thinkers do not waste time, but they make the most of their time. Does it make sense to invest your thoughts on something and not profit from it? Only fools make an investment and not look for a return. Jesus is the ultimate thinker, and He receives a return on His investment daily. He died so we may live, and as a result, many of us are going to join Him in Heaven one day. Thanks for the investment, Jesus! Do not invest your time focusing on issues you cannot change. A better investment is to focus on what you can change and control – yourself.

Do yourself a favor, and rationally reason with yourself before you do anything. Slow down. The highway of life can be very bumpy at times. For some strange reason, many of us seem to be in a rush these days. Because of this attitude, few of us have mastered the art of thought processing. We have become a society of reacting without deliberation. Making a mistake and correcting it will be costly as it demands even more of our precious time. Who among us can purchase one second of tomorrow? Are you a patient or an impatient person? A thinker must have mental endurance. Patience is the area where most of us fail. We do not take the "Time-Out" to contemplate the matter at hand from point "A" to point "Z." People blame their impatience on the microwave society. I personally believe that it is a matter of choices and not society. A real man accepts responsibility and does not play the blame game.

Reflect on the times that you made a rushed decision, and think about the results. If you could change three decisions you made and dedicate more time to them, which decisions would you choose? Patience is very beneficial for a thinker as it helps to purify the thinking process. "But let patience have its perfect work, that you may be perfect and complete, lacking nothing" {James 1:4NKJV}.

The area of patience was a weakness for me. That is why I make a daily effort to strengthen my mind by practicing more patience. A real man knows the importance of understanding the detailed complications of a situation and does not make a decision if he is anxious. I know the power of a thinking man, and I also know the power of a patient man. You cannot have one without the other as they go hand in hand. Issues can be very difficult to solve which is why you want to be the master of your thoughts. Mastering your thoughts leads to peace. There is nothing like remaining calm in the eye of the storm. Your woman is going to have even more love for you once she knows you are a patient thinker.

Let us examine this statement, "But as he was thinking this over." Thinking is something you do over, and over, and over again with lots of patience. You are going to excel in every area of your life once you become disciplined in your planning and thinking. It requires time to process life's battles, and patience is a vital weapon which secures your victories. Patience allows you to study the enemy, and by doing so, you will discover his weaknesses.

Agitation signifies a lack of patience. Can a union grow if patience is lacking? Perseverance is brain food. It feeds your mind healthy chemicals and improves your mentality. Thinkers endure constantly as they go the extra mile for the best results. God loves physical and spiritual fitness; therefore, it is His desire for us to be in great shape. "If someone forces you to go one mile, go with him two miles" {Matthew 5:41NIV}. The title "Thinker" is not given but has to be earned. It is earned by constant effort, dedication, and the ability to overcome difficult circumstances. Difficulties strengthen your mind, and a strong mind is always victorious in the face of life's challenges. Your ability to reason wisely will be rewarded. God rewards thinkers.

A real man understands the importance of policing his thoughts. "For as he thinks in his heart, so is he" {Proverbs 23:7NKJV}. A real man does not ignore negative thoughts but defeats negative thoughts with the Word of God. The Scriptures are your greatest defense against undesirable beliefs. The minute you apply the Scriptures to your mind, it begins to uproot the fruitless seeds which are planted and replaces them with fruitful seeds. You cannot live beyond your thought life. A properly trained mind experiences real success. Your mind is valuable. Nurture it. Invest in it. Your mind is your greatest asset. Constantly feed it the Word of God. We are attacked by negative thoughts daily, and we must defeat them daily in order to succeed in every area of our lives. An accumulation of negative thoughts produces an explosion that will not benefit anyone. We have learned the impact of a build-up; therefore, we must do what Jesus did the moment He was presented with negative thoughts by responding with the Word of God {Read Matthew Chapter 4:1-11}.

Have you ever been in a bad mood and suddenly heard your favorite song? Did you begin to sing the words of the song? Did the song change how you were feeling? Did you notice what happened to your mood as the song began to play? Self-talk is powerful. We all know the saying, "Sticks and stones may break my bones, but words will never hurt me." Deception comes to mind as I examine this statement. This belief is one of the biggest lies ever told. Wicked comments are responsible for more damages than many of us understand. Be mindful of the truth that your words are powerful. "You are snared with the words of your lips, you are caught by the speech of your mouth" {Proverbs 6:2AMP}. You must properly train your mouth in order to properly train your mind. The words you speak become images in your mind. For this reason, I am encouraging you to speak the Scriptures aloud as much as possible. A brilliant mind is feed and developed when God's word is planted into it. I once was a negative person who was easily ruled by my mental images. As I replaced the negative words that I spoke with the Scriptures, I conquered my negative thought life.

Imagine how a person with low self-esteem feels when he or she hears, "That is a beautiful dress. That color really looks nice on you. I love your hair. That perfume/cologne smells really good." Positive communications has the power to change someone's life. Words penetrate an individual's hearing, heart, mind, soul, and spirit. A real man is the master of conversation. He is patient and cleverly chooses his words.

I find this preparation to be a great way to start my day. Challenge yourself to spend the first ten minutes of your day declaring uplifting words aloud. Here is an example for you: "I am honoring the Lord today with my actions, thoughts, and words. I am a blessing to everyone with whom I come in contact. I am a man of patience. I am the master at making obedient decisions. I am a thinking man. I have the mind of Christ. I have a renewed mind. I love my woman. I will demonstrate my appreciation for her whenever I have the chance. I am choosing my words wisely today. I will speak to others as if I am speaking to the Creator Himself."

Do the same preparation ten minutes prior to going to bed, but state the words that pertain to the time of day. For example: "I am grateful because today I honored the Lord with my actions, thoughts, and words." Keeping your thoughts in proper alignment requires determination, skills, and lots of patience. If you do not control your thinking, it will eventually control you. "For though we live in the world, we do not wage war as the world does. The weapons we fight with are not the weapons of the world. On the contrary, they have divine power to demolish strongholds. We demolish arguments and every pretension that sets itself up against the knowledge of God, and we take captive every thought to make it obedient to Christ. And we will be ready to punish every act of disobedience, once your obedience is complete" {2nd Corinthians 10:3-6NIV}.

Do not limit yourself to the first and last ten minutes of your day. Please feel free to acknowledge God as much as possible. The more you honor Him, the more your mind will embrace His principles. I have a winner's mentality, and I give credit to the Creator, His principles, and His words. I recognize Him all day long by speaking the Scriptures to myself constantly, especially when I am in the car driving. I drive in silence, and I recite His word aloud. Your ability to think properly will get better by the day once you consistently perform this practice. Your woman will be very attracted to your renewed mind. "Do not conform any longer to the pattern of this world, but be transformed by the renewing of your mind" {Romans 12:2NIV}.

Ladies, how you think of your man is vital. How you treat him is a reflection of how you perceive him. You can always tell a woman who honors and appreciates her man by actions which reflect respect and gratitude. I know it may be difficult to have healthy thoughts of him if you are experiencing challenges in your relationship. However, if you are going to help him become a real man, you have to view him the way you would like for him to view you, or even better, see him the way God sees him. God's outlook of your man is as a winner. In the eyes of the Creator, your man is full of potential in spite of any flaws he has.

My wife displayed positive thoughts towards me, and her actions helped me to see myself differently. I can remember her always making pleasant remarks about me even though, I was not worthy of her praise. Eventually, I became the words that she was constantly speaking. You will believe and become what you continuously hear. The words she spoke drew many priceless photographs in my mind, and the images streamed into my heart. True change is not a condition of the mind as much as a condition of the heart. Think about how a lovely card has the ability to warm your heart. I recall a time when my wife gave me a card which read, "I was just thinking of you." It felt really good to know that she was affectionately thinking of me. Her thoughtfulness along with the words in the card encouraged me in my efforts. The powerful combination of loving thoughts and encouraging words sketched an unforgettable picture in my mind of unconditional love.

Get a vivid mental illustration of the life you desire for you both, and live in it. Everything in life happens twice. We first experience living in the invisible world of our thinking and then in the visible world as our thoughts become our reality. You need to initially capture your desired life in the unseen so you can own your desired life in the seen. Once you have a solid mental portrait, speak about the photo as much as possible. Let your man hear you describe the photograph, "I am so grateful that Rick is the master thinker. Rick makes great decisions pertaining to his life and our family. Everyone benefits from Rick's choices. Rick's thinking is in alignment with God's thinking. Rick has the mind of Christ." Do you see the power of your words? What sort of impact do you believe this encouragement will have on him? The statements you voice will give you both a lovely depiction of tomorrow. He may not show you his appreciation at first, but he eventually will. The words you speak will help "Rick" become a master thinker.

I was looking at a marathon one day and was very surprised by the outcome. There were two runners who separated themselves from the pack. The runner in first place had a huge lead over the second place runner. I observed how the leading runner kept looking behind while the runner in second place aimed his focus straight ahead. Amazingly, the runner in second place eventually caught up to the leader of the pack, and he won the race. I learned so much from watching this marathon. The leading runner ran his race backwards while the trailing runner focused on the finish line. When the winner was interviewed, he stated, "I kept saying to myself, I will win this race. I will see the finish line first despite of my position." I wonder what the leading runner was saying to himself as he kept looking behind. Let me encourage you to speak and think your relationship across the finish line. Do not focus on what has happened, but patiently focus on what will happen. "But Lot's wife looked back from behind him, and she became a pillar of salt" {Genesis 19:26AMP}. Lot's wife was not able to release her past; therefore, she was stuck in the past and never saw the dawn of a new day. Do not allow any past challenges to keep your relationship in darkness. Let them go. You are a winner. There is nothing but good things in store for you both. You cannot embrace your amazing future while you are holding onto your past.

Relationships are lots of work, and the people who succeed in their unions are the ones who endure to the very end. In this case, endurance does not pertain to physical abilities. It pertains to emotional, mental, and spiritual abilities. These supernatural abilities will not be in the life of a person who does not think properly. Think about what you and your man will receive once you both cross the finish line. Do you see the prize? Now, speak to him about it as much as you like.

Here is a prayer for you: Father, strengthen our thinking as "Rick" and I go through this journey. Uproot all thoughts that are hindering "Rick's" ability to think like Joseph. Bless us both with the mind of Christ. Supply us with the determination to complete this race. Teach us how to view each other as You view us. Thank You for renovating our minds. Thanks for helping us to see and experience Your love, in Jesus' name. Amen.

87

<u>Reflection</u>

Please take the time to journal your questions and comments as a powerful way to track your progress. These moments are when you take the time to reflect on what you have learned in this chapter and express your thoughts. What did you learn from this chapter? How do others perceive you? Are you viewed as a thinker? Are you recognized as a patient person? Are you good at speaking the right words at the right time? What steps are you going to take in order to become a master thinker? What steps are you going to take to increase your patience level? How can you improve your choice of words and the spirit that is attached to them? How important is your mind? How much time are you investing into it? What are you feeding your mind? What movies are you watching? What songs are you hearing? Who are your friends?

God and I want you to succeed. The question is how desperately do you want to succeed? In order to attain these values, you must devote one hundred percent to the journey. Ninety-nine percent will not get you to your destination. Your dedication must be rock solid in order for you to experience true success in your relationship. I compare this dedication to a funeral. You have to die to your old self so the new you can live. Habits are easy to form and hard to break. Practice these principles continuously, and the old ones will eventually perish. I believe in you. Keep pressing towards the finish line. Your reward will be great.

Here is a confession for you to pray: I am a man of excellence, and I excel in all that I do. I think big, and I get big results because I serve a big God. I go the extra mile with joy to honor God and my woman. I am a man of high standards just like Joseph, and I will maintain my standards no matter the circumstances. I am an overcomer; therefore, I succeed in all that I do. Thank You, Father, for helping me with this transformation. I am a real man, and I will demonstrate this stance daily, in Jesus' name. Amen.

See if you remember what you read in this chapter.

What do you need to possess in order to be a master thinker?

____ ____ ____ ____ ____ ____ ____ ____.

A Real Man Knows God

Matthew 1:20 But as he was thinking this over, behold, **an angel of the Lord appeared to him** in a dream, saying, Joseph, descendant of David, do not be afraid to take Mary {as} your wife, for that which is conceived in her is of {from, out of} the Holy Spirit.

A real man knows God. Joseph was certainly a man who knew the Lord and knew Him very well. His character and the control he displayed was proof of this awareness. God is our Author and the source of true transformation. You will not transform into a real man without His daily input. Everything you learn from this book will not work independently from the Creator since all of these principles are a reflection of Him. We need the Father and all that He has to offer. We are powerless without Him. Divine intervention is very much required.

"Anyone who listens to my teaching and follows it is wise, like a person who builds a house on solid rock. Though the rain comes in torrents and the floodwaters rise and the winds beat against that house, it won't collapse because it is built on bedrock. But anyone who hears my teaching and doesn't obey it is foolish, like a person who builds a house on sand. When the rains and floods come and the winds beat against that house, it will collapse with a mighty crash" {Matthew 7:24-27NLT}. A real man builds his foundation on the solid rock established by the Grand Architect and not the sinking sand designed by man.

Prayer, reading the Bible, or conversing with the Creator should not be something you do once in a while or when uneasiness emerges but should be done daily. A key principle is the more time you spend with the Creator, the more you will become like Him. There is nothing more attractive to a woman than a man who looks, reasons, speaks, and responds like God. You know you are transforming when your character begins to resemble the Lord. You must spend as much time as possible with the only Man who can change all men – Jesus. "Therefore, if anyone is in Christ, he is a new creation; old things have passed away; behold, all things have become new" {2nd Corinthians 5:17NKJV}.

You cannot become a real man without Jesus' input. He is "THE" example of a real man. A woman was naked, and He covered her {John 8:1-11}. A woman had an issue, and He helped her to solve it {Luke 8:43-48}. A woman needed a loving conversation, and He spoke to her {John 4:1-42}. Jesus shows us the importance of protecting all women.

A real man spends more time with the Lord than anyone or anything else. He is the source of a meaningful life. He is the foundation for establishing a fulfilling relationship with your lady. It is my belief that a man will not be able to have a healthy relationship with his woman without first having a healthy relationship with God. Do you believe any relationship would fail if it was handled the way that God handles our relationship with Him? Think about it. He never quits on us, leaves us alone, or divorces us. There is not another companion like Him. He will never lie to us, misguide us, or cheat on us. He is the best listener, and He always provides the best advice. Ever since Adam and Eve mistreated their relationship with Him, He has been diligently working towards rebuilding His bond with mankind. The Bible is the ultimate relationship book and the greatest love story ever written. It is also an ongoing connection between the unchanging love of the Father and His children. He is not only your Father and God, but He is also your best point of contact concerning all matters of life. I was blessed with this valuable understanding as I began to solidly build my union with the Creator. Lots of intimate "TIME" with the Father is required.

The burdens that I once carried were removed after I realized the true meaning of a loving relationship. God transformed my life by becoming whoever I needed Him to be. For instance, when I was spiritually sick, He became my spiritual Healer. When I felt weak, He became my Strength. When I was confused, He became my Teacher. He will never ask you to do something that cannot be done. He will always give you the strength, determination, and example of someone who has already accomplished a similar task. My conversion is totally credited to the Transformer and His principles. He changed me, taught me how to be a real man, and is the reason why this book is written. My wife, family, friends, society, and I are benefiting from the link I have with the Lord. Your association with Him will be reflected in the connections you have with others. There is no way you can have a patient, loving, caring, and respectful relationship with the Creator and have the opposite relationship with people. He expects you to treat individuals the way you would like to be treated. "So then, whatever you desire that others would do to and for you, even so do also to and for them, for this is {sums up} the Law and the Prophets" {Matthew 7:12AMP}.

People are able to recognize your affiliation to God by your attitude, conversations, and the love you display. A real man is not ashamed or afraid to express his love for Jesus. Do not be embarrassed or fearful, but rather be "BOLD" about the feelings you have for Jesus. If you are uncomfortable or scared in expressing your passion for Christ, you will be uncomfortable or scared in expressing your passion for your woman. If shame or fear is present, love is missing. There is no shame or fear in love. This empowering emotion grants us all the freedom to freely express ourselves.

One question forever changed my life, and I believe it will do the same for you. I asked the Lord one day, "Why are You invisible to us?" He responded, "I desire to perfect your ability to love." Wow, this statement was life changing. If you love the Creator whom you have not seen, you should be able to love your brother or sister whom you see. "We love Him because He first loved us. If someone says, "I love God," and hates his brother, he is a liar; for he who does not love his brother whom he has seen, how can he love God whom he has not seen? And this commandment we have from Him: that he who loves God must love his brother also" {1st John 4:19-21NKJV}.

As stated earlier, a real man must go through a transformation. However, God has to be the source of the transformation. There is no transformation without God. The change resembles a caterpillar that goes into a cocoon and emerges as a butterfly. As the caterpillar goes into the cocoon, it is contained in a dark place. At that point, the caterpillar begins to die to the old creation so that the new creature may live. True change happens internally and requires some form of death. Remember, something old must die in order for something new to live. After the conversion, the caterpillar has a new name {butterfly}, it looks different {beautiful colors}, and it is able to function differently. The new creature is no longer crawling but is able to fly. This transforming process is what a real man experiences.

True change occurs from the inside out. A real man lives his life internally and not externally. Living in this fashion is not easy, but it can be done. You may be thinking, "That was Joseph. This lifestyle is impossible. I cannot live the way he did." I stated earlier in this chapter that God will always give you the strength, determination, and example of someone who has already accomplished a similar task. Joseph is the example who the

Creator has given us. Joseph is the model for us to see true manhood. You can do it! You can do whatever you put your mind to understand and believe. Please understand that transformation is not a one-time activity but rather is a daily progression.

Like the butterfly fighting its way out of the cocoon, you must fight daily for your transformation and relationship. Do not become relaxed because of yesterday's victories, but utilize them as daily motivations for accomplishing your everyday goals. David won his battle with Goliath by reflecting on his past victories. "And David said to Saul, Your servant kept his father's sheep. And when there came a lion or again a bear and took a lamb out of the flock, I went out after it and smote it and delivered the lamb out of its mouth; and when it arose against me, I caught it by its beard and smote it and killed it. Your servant killed both the lion and the bear; and this uncircumcised Philistine shall be like one of them, for he has defied the armies of the living God! David said, The Lord Who delivered me out of the paw of the lion and out of the paw of the bear, He will deliver me out of the hand of this Philistine. And Saul said to David, Go, and the Lord be with you!" {1st Samuel 17:34-37AMP}.

Remember that preparation is the key to real success. You should not wait for a battle to appear and then go into training. A real man is always prepared. Preparation is the way to protect your woman and children.

My makeover was not easy at all, but I continuously relied on the Lord. The more time I spent with Him, the stronger and more determined I became. Like a butterfly, the transition gave me a new look and a new way to live. During my transformation, three different butterflies flew into the palm of my hand on three different occasions. On one of those occasions, I was blessed to stroke the butterfly with my pointer finger. I know that this miracle was a true gift from God. Spend time with the Creator, and let the renovation begin. You will experience life on a whole different level.

Ladies, I am often asked, "How do I know if he is a good man?" The more time you spend with Jesus, the easier it is for you to identify a good man. Jesus is the ultimate Gentleman, and His qualities are irresistible. Here are the characteristics of Jesus and a good man: love, joy, peace, patience, kindness, goodness, faithfulness, gentleness, and self-control.

As we have discussed, life is lived from the inside out. If these values are within you, they eventually will come out of you. What values do you hold dearly to your heart? These values represent the kind of man you will attract. What type of man charms your imaginations? Your heart is the home of your imaginations which influences your desires. Your desires are like a strong magnetic force. For this reason, I am suggesting for you to step up your level of intimacy with Jesus. He will satisfy your cravings. Therefore, your taste buds will not be satisfied with a man who lacks the fruit of the Spirit which are the nine characteristics in the previous paragraph. Have you ever heard the saying, "Birds of a feather flock together?" Have you ever seen an eagle hanging around a pigeon?

Talk to Jesus daily, eat with Him, read His word, listen to His instructions, and ask for His input in all matters. Even sing to Him. After you go out on a rendezvous with Jesus, go out with the man of your interests. At that moment, you will see who he really is. During your time with Jesus, you will experience so much kindness. How many people would you have avoided if this understanding was your measuring stick?

Spending time with Jesus elevates your standards. You should expect the best because you are the best. Many women choose the wrong type of man believing that they are no good men. You are better off alone instead of settling. Have you ever had a craving for something only to eat something else? Did your second option satisfy you? Do not settle. A man can sense if a woman has low standards, and he will give her exactly what she expects. Let him know about the first man in your life {Jesus} in order for him to become the second man in your life.

My wife started to spend lots of time with Jesus, and it sparked my curiosity. Honestly, the attention that she gave to Jesus provoked me to jealousy. It is amazing how God would use the emotion of envy for my good. The question echoed in my mind, "Why does she have more interest in Jesus than me?" This curiosity inspired me to learn more about the MAN who had her heart, and in turn, I began to emulate the Person I was studying. Now, do you see the importance of knowing the Lord? Because of the relationship that my wife established with the Creator, I now know Him. Honoring God is going to either draw you two closer together or push you two further apart. Whether you grow closer together or further apart is how you will know if he is a decent man for you.

Here is a prayer for you: Father, teach me Your ways. I desire to learn more about You. Give "Darnell" and I a zeal for you like never before. Communicate to "Darnell" the importance of spending more time with You. I pray that as we both seek You, we will learn how to please You in our relationship. I desire a higher level of intimacy with You. I promise to spend more time with You from this day forward. "Darnell" and I must build our home on a strong foundation based on You and Your word, and we will. Thanks for helping us to raise our values to Your values, in Jesus' name. Amen.

Reflection

Please take the time to journal your questions and comments as a powerful way to track your progress. These moments are when you take the time to reflect on what you have learned in this chapter and express your thoughts. What did you learn from this chapter? How would you rate your relationship with God: poor, fair, good, or great? What role does He play in your daily life? How much time do you spend with Him? Do you have an established time arranged for you and the Lord to intimately communicate with each other? Do you spend more time watching television, on the phone, or on social networking sites than you do with the Creator? Are you able to express the love you have for Him to others? How important is it for you to please Him? What can you do to better your connection with Him?

You will perfect your relationship with your woman and children as you begin to perfect your relationship with God. I am not describing "perfect" in the natural sense. I am describing "perfect" in the spiritual sense. "You, therefore, must be perfect {growing into complete maturity of godliness in mind and character, having reached the proper height of virtue and integrity}, as your heavenly Father is perfect" {Matthew 5:48AMP}. Note your progress daily, and reflect on your achievements weekly. The consistency in your behavior will motivate you. Your woman will begin to evolve as well. Progression is challenging and rewarding all at the same time.

Here is a confession for you to pray: I am a man of excellence, and I excel in all that I do. I think big, and I get big results because I serve a big God. I go the extra mile with joy to honor God and my woman. I am a man of high standards just like Joseph, and I will maintain my standards no matter the circumstances. I am an overcomer; therefore, I succeed in all that I do. Thank You, Father, for helping me with this transformation. I am a real man, and I will demonstrate this stance daily, in Jesus' name. Amen.

See if you remember what you read in this chapter.

What will you be like when you emerge from your transformation?

____ ____ ____ ____ ____ ____ ____ ____ ____.

A Real Man Is a Dreamer

Matthew 1:20 But as he was thinking this over, behold, an angel of the Lord appeared to him **in a dream**, saying, Joseph, descendant of David, do not be afraid to take Mary {as} your wife, for that which is conceived in her is of {from, out of} the Holy Spirit {Amplified Bible}.

A real man sleeps in the midst of issues even though they may be challenging. Joseph was weighing his options and seeking wisdom in his sleep. Some of the answers you are pursuing have not yet been revealed to you due to a lack of slumber. Sleeping is one the best methods to employ when you are confronted with challenges. It is a way of clearing your mind allowing God to speak to you as He spoke to Joseph. How many times have you pressed through a problem knowing you should have been resting instead? What was the result of your forceful action? Can you make sound choices if you are not rested?

Decisions direct a person's life in one way or the other. It is best to make a decision with a refreshed mind. A tired mind does not process as well as a reenergized one. Resting does not mean you ignore the issues. Resting means you allow yourself the time to strengthen your focus so you can take the appropriate actions as Joseph did. A good night's rest works very well for people when they are in need of answers. Resting during problematic situations displays confidence and is reassuring. Your woman will certainly appreciate your calm demeanor. Your actions speak. Your decision to sleep instead of worrying says, "I believe it is all going to work out in the end. This issue is not beyond repair. I am going to control what I can and let go of what I cannot." Your calmness demonstrates discipline, mental toughness, and self-control. A real man is able to sleep in the face of adversity. The storm does not control him, but rather he controls the storm.

"On that same day {when} evening had come, He said to them, let us go over to the other side {of the lake}. And leaving the throng, they took Him with them, {just} as He was, in the boat {in which He was sitting}. And other boats were with Him. And a furious storm of wind {of hurricane proportions} arose, and the waves kept beating into the boat, so that it was already becoming filled. But He {Himself} was in the stern {of the boat}, asleep on the {leather} cushion; and they awoke Him and said to Him, Master, do You not care that we are perishing? And He arose and rebuked the wind and said to the sea, Hush now! Be still {muzzled}! And the wind ceased {sank to rest as if exhausted by its beating} and there was {immediately a great calm {a perfect peacefulness}" {Mark 4:35-39AMP}.

A real man maintains his composure no matter the condition. I cannot stress enough the importance of controlling the storms of life. I suggest you find a resting place if something is troubling you. When I have a battle to deal with or feel agitated, I try to completely relax. While I am relaxing, I have a conversation with God. I say, "Father, I have a situation here, and I do not have the answer for it, but You do. I trust You, and I thank You in advance for solving this dilemma for me. I have complete trust in You; therefore, I am going to sit back, relax, and rest this secured confidence. You are the answer to all conflicts, and You are my strength regardless of the issues. I am holding onto my joy because this problem is already solved, in Jesus' name. Amen." You do not have to die in order to "Rest in Peace." You can rest in peace while you are alive. You are learning how to rest in peace so start practicing now.

Joseph slept, and the Creator answered him. Make use of this approach, and He will answer you. Believe it or not, the Lord wants us to rest. When we are resting, He is working on our behalf. "And the Lord God caused a deep sleep to fall upon Adam; and while he slept, He took one of his ribs or a part of his side and closed up the {place with} flesh. And the rib or part of his side which the Lord God had taken from the man He built up and made into a woman, and He brought her to the man. Then Adam said, this {creature} is now bone of my bones and flesh of my flesh; she shall be called Woman, because she was taken out of a man" {Genesis 2:21-23AMP}.

The solutions which we are seeking are within us. Strangely enough, many of us are looking outwardly instead of inwardly. Imagine searching for your keys while they are in your pocket. I have turned my house upside down looking for my keys only to discover that they were in my pocket. We must rest as Adam did. Once we are able to rest as Adam did, God will bless us as He blessed Adam. God always has your best interests, and He will always help you settle your concerns. Will you let Him? Again, He needs your permission to get involved in your life, and once you invite Him in, the problems are solved. "He said, Hearken, all Judah, you inhabitants of Jerusalem, and you King Jehoshaphat. The Lord says this to you: Be not afraid or dismayed at this great multitude; for the battle is not yours, but God's" {2nd Chronicles 20:15AMP}. Having intimate communications with the Lord is a form of resting and is necessary.

I had numerous sleepless nights in the past, and the lack of sleep produced tension. I transferred the agitation to my wife which only made matters worse. My confidence in God was not what it is today. Therefore, I wanted to be in control instead of trusting Him to help me with the troubling circumstances. I am so glad the sleepless nights are a thing of the past, and I am resting with so much ease now. I have unwavering faith in the Creator, and it works. I refuse to be stressed. Having an intimate relationship with God is essential for many reasons. One reason is that it allows you to live a stress free life. I am not saying you will not have challenges, but the relationship ensures that the challenges will not have you.

A real man has an amazing imagination and the ability to dream big. Dreaming is a gift from God, and yet, many of us have abandoned this gift. A real man dreams when his eyes are closed and when his eyes are open. The ability to dream and live in that place requires loyal faith. Dreams are the destination for the impossible, and the impossible is where the Lord works the best. The Creator loves it when we reach and aim high. "But without faith it is impossible to please and be satisfactory to Him. For whoever would come near to God must {necessarily} believe that God exists and that He is the rewarder of those who earnestly and diligently seek Him {out}" {Hebrews 11:6AMP}.

Women love to dream. Sit with your woman and imagine the perfect life. Ask her this question, "When you think of the perfect life what do you see?" At that point, add to the mental portrait she is painting. If she is visualizing having children, discuss their names, the color of their rooms, and the style of their strollers. If she foresees a home, discuss the furniture, curtains, and paint colors. She has been dreaming her entire life. Her dreams consist of the perfect wedding, the seamless marriage, the impeccable husband, the unflawed children, and the picture-perfect career. Ask about her vision of happily ever after and watch the smile appear on her face and the glow in her eyes. Dreaming is something she does all of the time, and once she knows you both are on the same page, she is going to love sharing her dreams with you.

Chose a weekly time when you both can dream together. Believe it or not, dreaming adds intimacy to your relationship and is just plain fun. Your dreams will eventually become your physical reality. There is nothing impossible for a dreamer because "all things can be {are possible} to him who believes" {Mark 9:23AMP}. God is limited in the life of a person who refuses to dream. Look at what He told Abram who was an old man. "The Lord said to Abram after Lot had left him, Lift up now your eyes and look from the place where you are, northward and southward and eastward and westward; for all the land which you see I will give to you and to your posterity forever. And I will make your descendants like the dust of the earth, so that if a man could count the dust of the earth, then could your descendants also be counted. Arise; walk through the land, the length of it and the breadth of it, for I will give it to you" {Genesis 13:14-17AMP}.

In this conversation, the Creator is provoking Abram to see beyond what his natural eyes can grasp. You have to dream big in order to believe you can have children long after the reproductive capability is gone. Abram was seventy-five years of age when he was mentally impregnated by God's vision that he would produce children. Giving birth to your dreams can be just as challenging as giving birth to a child. For this reason, you must push beyond what you are feeling. You will never live outside of your imagination or further than your dreams. Notice how many times God said, "I will." God expressed His will to Abram three times in that one conversation. You can learn a lot from this discussion. First, God's will is greater than your feelings. Second, embrace the vision that God has placed in your heart. Faith does not make sense, and sense does not make faith. These are two opposite ways of living.

In the New Testament of the Bible, Zacharias is introduced as an elderly man. God reveals to him that he would become a father, and Zacharias doubts God's vision, and as a result, God is forced to silence him during his wife's pregnancy. Zacharias and Abram were both old in age as were their wives. The difference between both men was that Abram embraced the Creator's vision while Zacharias doubted {Read Genesis Chapter 15:1-6}. The Lord had to mute Zacharias voice so that His plan would be manifested {Read Luke Chapter 1:5-25}. You must have the faith that Abraham showed in trusting the Word of God to make the impossible possible.

When God informed Mary of her virgin birth, she had an obedient and faithful response. "Then Mary said, "Behold the maidservant of the Lord! Let it be to me according to your word." And the angel departed from her" {Luke Chapter 1:26-38NKJV}. You have to be a dreamer in order to experience God's will for your life.

Reflect on how Dr. Martin Luther King, Jr. had a dream a long time ago, and we are still benefiting from that dream today. There is nothing you can do to stop a dreamer. A dream cannot be stopped. Albert Einstein stated, "Imagination is more important than knowledge." God said, "For as he thinks in his heart so is he" {Proverbs 23:7NKJV}. A real man goes into his place of rest and dreams big while he is resting.

I have been a dreamer my entire life, I always wanted more out of my existence, and I constantly saw myself making it big in every sense of the word. However, the many obstructions that I faced blocked my vision, and I struggled not to lose my ability to dream big. It is very important for you to free yourself from all negativity. You will not be able to dream as the Lord desires without this freedom. Seeking the Lord became very beneficial. He is the reason why my dreams are now a reality. He removed all of the darkness and gave me His light to follow. Now, my mind is occupied with unlimited potentials. When I lift up my eyes, I see more stars than I can count. The stars signify endless opportunities. Do you know that you possess endless opportunities? What would you do if you knew you could not fail? How would you approach life if you knew success was inevitable?

Consider yourself a farmer, and your thoughts are the seeds which eventually sprout and harvest. You cannot plant an apple seed and receive a grape harvest. Every seed reproduces after its own kind. God said, "Let the land sprout with vegetation—every sort of seed-bearing plant, and trees that grow seed-bearing fruit. These seeds will then produce the kinds of plants and trees from which they came" {Genesis 1:11NLT}. Your seeds are the positive or negative thoughts that you carry daily.

Because of these life changing principles, I am able to dream and experience my deepest desires. This book was once a dream of mine, and now it exists. Thank You, Lord! I give all of the credit to God. He thought me how to reprogram my mind, and now, I am not only dreaming, but I am thinking big, beyond what this world has ever seen. Your divine visions are your spiritual reality, and they become your physical reality once you are able to see life from God's point of view. Dream big, my friend. The best is yet to come.

Ladies, encourage your man to get as much rest as possible by creating a pleasant environment for him. Cook him a nice meal, light a candle, play relaxing music, give him a massage, and encourage him with your words. Your thoughtful attention will be soothing to him. As you well know, stress adds tension to the body and mind. With your help, the negative atmosphere will change, the anxiety will flee, and he will get his well-needed rest.

Pray for your man while he is asleep. I can remember waking up as my wife was wide awake praying for me. I did not understand why she was praying so I asked her, "Why are you praying?" She said, "Your spirit is not at peace. I am praying for God to give you the comfort you need." I did not comprehend her words then; however, I see her rational now. She wanted my spirit to be calm so I could lead effectively and point our family in the right direction. Remember, your man is the leader of the family. If he is stressed, he will not lead effectively and point your family in the right direction. My wife's prayers lifted my spirit, and the results were just amazing. Other than God, you are your man's main supporter. If he is not able to guard your home due to stress, you must stand guard. If the environment in your home is not peaceful, the both of you will not be able to rest or dream. For this reason, I give you a prayer. Please read these prayers aloud to create the right atmosphere in your home. Repetition is vital as it increases your faith. You will believe what you continually hear. "So then faith comes by hearing, and hearing by the word of God" {Romans 10:17NKJV}. Knowing is half of the battle. Action is required. Apply this truth daily, and you will see the results of your deepest dreams. It is so wonderful to be connected to a partner who has your back, front, and sides. Your man will feed off of your energy due to your confidence and dedication. Stress has a way of robbing us of our faith if we let it, but prayer eliminates all stressful moments.

Never underestimate the power of your words. Encourage your man with your loving words. This encouragement is not limited to him being in your presence. Your thoughts and words are alive. They will inspire him whether he is with you or not. As "there is no distance in prayer," no distance in thoughts, and no distance in your caring comments. You are created in the image and likeness of God. Therefore, you have the power to operate the way He operates. The Creator created the world and everything in it by the power of His words. In the beginning, the earth was dark and empty, and God spoke light into the earth. You can speak light into your relationship whenever darkness presents itself, and as a result, the light appears, and the darkness flees. "In the beginning God {prepared, formed, fashioned, and} created the heavens and the earth. The earth was without form and an empty waste, and darkness was upon the face of the very great deep. The Spirit of

God was moving {hovering, brooding} over the face of the waters. And God said, Let there be light; and there was light" {Genesis 1:1-3AMP}.

If you are alive, you should be pursuing your dreams. Pursue your dreams with all of your heart, soul, and strength. Many of us believe it is too late to accomplish our dreams due to our age. Remember Abraham. God did not give up on Abraham's dream of becoming a father. God has not given up on you because of your age. In reality, it took twenty five years for Abraham to receive what God promised him. He was one hundred years old when his son Isaac was born {Read Genesis 17:17-21}. Dream big! Is outer space not beyond the view of the sky? Has man not walked on the moon? Question whether the sky is the limit if you can travel beyond it. Our thoughts are mental pictures, and we are in control of the images and the paint that we allow on the canvases of our mind. Your dreams are a gift from the Lord. Do not allow anyone or anything to rob you of your visions.

Here is a prayer for you: Father, I have authority over this atmosphere because I am created in Your image and likeness. Therefore, I am commanding a peaceful environment for "Anderson" and me, and I speak Your peace into his spirit. "Anderson" is at rest, his spirit is empowered, and he is dreaming us into our amazing future. I am thankful that "Anderson" and I have the same vision. I am grateful for the ability to rest comfortably. "Anderson," me, and our children are experiencing the results of answered prayers, in Jesus' name. Amen.

Reflection

Please take the time to journal your questions and comments as a powerful way to track your progress. These moments are when you take the time to reflect on what you have learned in this chapter and express your thoughts. What did you learn from this chapter? Are you able to sleep when you are faced with issues? When you are frustrated, do you rest or press through the frustration? Do you worry easily? Are you a visionary? How important is dreaming to you? What is your perfect life? What are you doing to capture your perfect life? Have you buried a God given vision? What do you need to do to resurrect this divine vision? Sleep and dream big while maintaining your faith.

Here is a confession for you to pray: I am a man of excellence, and I excel in all that I do. I think big, and I get big results because I serve a big God. I go the extra mile with joy to honor God and my woman. I am a man of high standards just like Joseph, and I will maintain my standards no matter the circumstances. I am an overcomer; therefore, I succeed in all that I do. Thank You, Father, for helping me with this transformation. I am a real man, and I will demonstrate this stance daily, in Jesus' name. Amen.

See if you remember what you read in this chapter.

How many times did God express His will to Abram during their conversation?

_____ _____ _____ _____ _____.

A Real Man Is Secure In His Identity

Matthew 1:20 But as he was thinking this over, behold, an angel of the Lord appeared to him in a dream, saying, **Joseph, descendant of David,** do not be afraid to take Mary {as} your wife, for that which is conceived in her is of {from, out of} the Holy Spirit {Amplified Bible}.

How do you view yourself? Do you see yourself as a king? It is very important for you to have the right image of yourself. If you do not acknowledge the king in you, you will not acknowledge the queen in your woman. You must know who you are.

A real man knows who he is and is secure in his identity and manhood. Joseph knew exactly who he was and was secure in his identity and manhood. He knew his blood line was traced to royalty {"descendant of David"}. Do you know who you are? Are you aware of the truth that your blood line is traced to royalty {Jesus}? "And on His garment {robe} and on His thigh He has a name {title} inscribed, King of Kings and Lord of Lords" {Revelation 19:16AMP}. A woman would rather be with a confident man more so than an insecure man.

A confident man is a secure man who represents safety. Remember, security is the most important quality your woman needs. Joseph was not abusive in any sense of the word to Mary despite what they faced. Imagine how attractive his actions were to her. She knew then that God had blessed her with "A Real MAN."

Confidence is always attached to joy. Women love joy. It is an irresistible feeling. It positively adds to their lives. It makes them feel good. Who does not like to feel good? Who wants to be around negative feelings? Undesirable spirits are thieves who rob you of your gladness. Would you trust an individual to protect you if he did not display confidence? How would you feel around a soldier or police officer who was not confident?

A real man confidently stands on his own two feet. He is not defined by material possessions. He is a real man with or without material objects. Lots of men base their manhood on the amount of money they have, the car they drive, or the house they own. Your manhood should not be measured by the amount of items you can accumulate. What happens if you can no longer accumulate these items? What happens to your manhood at that point? "Those who love money will never have enough. How meaningless to think that wealth brings true happiness" {Ecclesiastes 5:10NLT}.

Material things do not validate or complete you. You are an incomplete man if this false sense of security is your belief, and there is no rest for an incomplete man. Chasing after material items, fame, and fortune is very tiresome, and it will have a toll on you. If you chase after these things, you will never be satisfied with who you are and what you have. I am a witness! The chase is an endless race without winners, and in the process, you will neglect your woman. Is she not more valuable than material possessions? You can always purchase things, but you cannot purchase a virtuous woman. A noble woman is priceless {Read Proverbs 31}.

A real man's identity is not attached to things that are replaceable. Material objects lose value and can be taken away. Have you ever noticed how quickly something new becomes something old? The feeling of new rapidly wears off when it is attached to material items; however, the feeling of new last forever when it pertains to spiritual items. I have purchased a new home, new vehicles, and new clothing only to lose the excitement after a short period of time. On the other hand, I am amazed how I still have the feeling of new for my wife and our marriage after all of this time. I am still excited about her every day, and our relationship is growing daily. When I first met her, I thought I loved her, but I now know love can be so much deeper. My attention now is aimed towards her heart and spirit even though she is also physically beautiful. A real man attaches himself to the spiritual side of the people in his life. The hearts of the people in your life are priceless, and you are privileged to share their hearts as long as you appreciate them. A real man's identity is attached to God and God only. Can anyone or anything take God away from you? Joseph found his identity in the Lord, and you should also.

I was once attached to material things, and I tried to convince myself that I was complete and happy because of my possessions. Deep down on the inside, I knew the truth. I was completely miserable and living a total lie. I was never satisfied with what I had or truly confident in myself. I had to have more of everything which negatively impacted my outlook on life. Now, I am proud to say that my identity is in the Creator and in the Creator only. Because of my security in my manhood, I have rebuilt what was once destroyed. There is nothing more valuable to me than the relationships that I have with the Lord, my wife, and my children. I am no longer uncertain about who I am. I know who I am with or without material objects. I am secure in myself, and I really feel good in my skin. The confidence I now have has worked wonders for me because my focus is no longer on me. My attention is directed at pleasing God first and then my wife.

If you are not a confident man, your attention is on you all of the time. When you are the center of your focus, it produces selfishness. On the other hand, if you are a confident man, your focus directs you towards your woman's needs. When the emphasis is on her, you are "holding down the fort." Selfishness or insecurities spotlights "me, myself, and I," but confidence focuses on the needs of others. Now do you see the importance of knowing who you are and being secure in your manhood?

113

It is often stated, "You complete me." This statement sounds like a good line; however, it is really a terrible way of thinking. You must be complete on your own. Do not expect your woman to complete you because she cannot. The Lord is the only one who can satisfy your emptiness. He is your Manufacturer and Foreman, and with your permission, He will assist you with your inner construction. He is the Supplier of all of your needs. "And my God will liberally supply {fill to the full} your every need according to His riches in glory in Christ Jesus" {Philippians 4:19AMP}. He is the missing ingredient in so many lives, and as a result, quite a few homes are falling apart.

Your woman can only be who the Creator created her to be. God did not create her to complete you. He created her to support you. The truth is she may also need to be completed. Stop! Save yourself the headache by not attempting to complete her because you cannot. You must have an established sense of self-confidence in order for your relationship to flourish and produce. If you do not know who you are, you are robbing you and your woman of a great experience.

It is often stated, "A relationship is fifty – fifty." This statement sounds impressive; however, it is wrong. A successful relationship is one hundred – one hundred. You have to bring one hundred percent to the relationship or marriage in order for it to work and thrive. Anything less adds unwanted stress and weight to the relationship. When you are one hundred percent complete and she is one hundred percent complete, you have a complete whole. This belief is the oneness God speaks about in the Bible concerning marriage. "But from the beginning of creation God made them male and female. For this reason a man shall leave {behind} his father and his mother and be joined to his wife and cleave closely to her permanently, and the two shall become one flesh, so that they are no longer two, but one flesh. What therefore

God has united {joined together}, let not man separate or divide" {Mark 10:6-9AMP}.

Let us take a closer look at this Scripture, "And the two shall become one flesh, so that they are no longer two, but one flesh." We have been taught that it is okay to give fifty percent in a relationship. This teaching has produced many divorces and broken homes. Another teaching we have embraced is the man's fifty percent plus the woman's fifty percent equals one hundred percent. We have even sung this song with so much passion: "Said now 70-30 – Now 60-40 – Talkin' 'bout a 50-50 love – yeah" {RIP Teddy Pendergrass}. The Lord never intended for us to experience marriage in this fashion. We have accepted a false truth, and as a result, the divorce rate is alarming. He stated, "And the two shall become one flesh." The truth is if you bring fifty percent to the relationship and your wife brings fifty percent to the relationship, you both have fifty percent in the marriage. For this reason, we have marriages missing fifty percent. Remember, the moment you are married, you become one. Therefore, if you both bring one hundred percent to the relationship, you both have one hundred percent once you are married. You and your wife are now lost in each other like grains of sand. If you both dropped a grain of sand in a glass full of sand, you would not be able to distinguish your sand from her sand. In marriage, you both have one heartbeat, one spirit, and one soul. Have you ever sensed when something was wrong with your wife? Have you ever felt the same discomforts she may have been feeling? Have you ever finished her statements? There are times that I know what my wife is feeling. We both experienced the same symptoms while she was pregnant. These experiences are not an accident. God designed these supernatural experiences.

Do not get married until you are one hundred percent sure of yourself. Remember, this confidence cannot come from you. It must come from the Creator. Your identity must be wrapped up in Him. When you are wrapped up in Him, you are lacking nothing. You are complete. At that point, you are ready to experience the joy of a successful marriage. Once you are complete on your own, you can avoid being added to the divorce statistic. Adam was not accompanied by Eve when he was created. He spent isolated time with God, and then he was able to meet his God given wife. This strategic time alone with God established Adam's completeness. The man was lacking nothing. Even the woman who God created for Adam was made from the inside of him {Read Genesis 2}. This illustration is powerful. It proves that the Creator has completed every one of us from the very beginning, but without Him, we are incomplete.

You will not be able to operate in your role as a husband if you are not secure in your identity. Do you know what your role is in your marriage? "And the Lord God took the man and put him in the Garden of Eden to tend and guard and keep it." {Genesis 2:15AMP}. Your role is to tend, guard, and keep everyone and everything in your Garden of Eden secure. You must symbolize security in every sense of the word. This role is easy to perform once you know who you are.

Give your burdens to Jesus by faith, and you or your wife will not have to deal with them any longer. Jesus said, "Casting the whole of your care {all your anxieties, all your worries, all your concerns, once and for all} on Him, for He cares for you affectionately and cares about you watchfully" {1st Peter 5:7AMP}. The man is commanded to love his wife as Christ loved the church. "For husbands, this means love your wives, just as Christ loved the church. He gave up his life for her" {Ephesians 5:25NLT}. That is why a godly man is a real man. He is willing to live a sacrificial life by honoring God and his woman. A man must know who he is and be composed in that place of knowing in order to operate by these principles.

My wife called me with an issue, and she was very upset. I listened intensely to her and expressed my deepest concern. Instantly, I began to think about a solution. I reassured her that the issue was going to be resolved, and I ended the conversation with a prayer. At that point, I felt the anxiety depart from her. I asked her to call me once everything was over, and I continued to pray for her peace and success while giving the situation to Jesus. Shortly after, she called me back with her praise report. If I were not confident in my identity, I would have handled this situation differently. I know that God is my Father, and I am His son. Thank You, Jesus!

Ladies, do not let your motherly instincts get in the way. You do not complete your man, and there is nothing you can do to complete him. You will be totally miserable if you attempt this task. Balance is needed. If your motherly instincts do get in the way, you will be in God's way. This approach will make matters worse due to the needless pressures. Yes, it is good to know who we are; however, it is very important to know who God is and His role in our lives as a whole.

These are the words of Adam the moment he met Eve, "At last!" the man exclaimed. "This one is bone from my bone, and flesh from my flesh! She will be called "woman," because she was taken from "man" {Genesis 2:23NLT}. This conversation confirmed Eve's identity and role in the marriage as the "Suitable Helper." Your position and identity is identical to Eve's role as "Suitable Helper." This arrangement places you beside your husband as his equal even though God intends for the man to lead. That is why it is vital for you to know who you are and your role as a loving wife.

As his helper, you are to encourage, honor, and respect your man at all times.

Ladies, when we think of finances, the traditional roles have changed. Quite a few women are now the major bread winners in their family. If this position pertains to you, you should not make your man feel as if he is not a king in your home. Remember, you both are a team, and there are other areas where he can be extremely helpful. Would these suggestions be accommodating to you? He can help by washing clothes, cleaning the house, helping with the children, and cooking the meals, etc. Regardless of his current financial situation, he needs to know that he is still a king in your home and in your eyes. A man can supply you with unlimited funds, and you can still have a troublesome relationship or marriage. Money cannot replace a caring, loving, and nurturing man.

I have heard it stated quite a few times, "Defense wins championships." When the basketball is stolen, the game becomes more exciting. This excitement is what your man feels as you are stealing the ball {obstacles} and helping him to score. Your defense and assist does not allow him to quit but to play to the very end and win. Where would a basketball team be without a great point guard? Where would a relationship be without an assisting woman? Never underestimate your role as your man's "Suitable Helper." If this role was not of importance, God would not have given it to Eve. Everything God gives us is a loving gift. Therefore, you are a loving gift to your man. "Two are better than one, because they have a good {more satisfying} reward for their labor; for if they fall, the one will lift up his fellow. But woe to him who is alone when he falls and has not another to lift him up! Again, if two lie down together, then they have warmth; but how can one be warm alone? And though a man might prevail against him who is alone, two will withstand him. A threefold cord is not quickly broken" {Ecclesiastes 4:9-12AMP}.

When the Angel spoke to Joseph he addressed him by his identity, "descendant of David." When you speak to your man, you should address him by his identity. "You are a man of wisdom. You are a loving and caring man. You are a great provider. You are the 2nd king in this house because Jesus is the 1st King in this house." Do you see the power in supporting his identity? The word "You" in this reinforcement is vital. It directs his attention to look within himself and not rely on you to give him his identity.

Do you know who you are? If you do not know who you are, you cannot expect for others to know who you are. You must present your king with a queen. You cannot treat your man like a king if you are not viewing yourself as a queen. Say this affirmation aloud: "I am a queen to my king. I am beautiful. I am intelligent. I know how to treat my king. I am a woman of excellence. I am a woman of truth. I am the sunlight on a cloudy day. I am the calm in the midst of all storms. I am sexy. I am patient. I am love. I am woman." How do you feel now?

Here is a prayer for you: Father, thank You for teaching me who I am in You. I am a queen, and "Phil" is my king. Thank You for helping us to recognize that we are royalty and that our identity is not determined by things or by people. Our identity is in You. Thank You for giving "Phil" the character of King Jesus. Thank You for teaching "Phil" how to lead as Jesus led. Teach me how to support "Phil" with everything he needs. Grant me the required wisdom to rule with "Phil" as You created our relationship to be. Teach "Phil" how to appreciate and honor my role as his "Suitable Helper," in Jesus' name. Amen.

Reflection

Please take the time to journal your questions and comments as a powerful way to track your progress. These moments are when you take the time to reflect on what you have learned in this chapter and express your thoughts. What did you learn from this chapter? Do you know who you are? Who are you? Do you need the approval of others to validate you? Are you incomplete because you do not have everything you desire? How are you going to exhibit attractive confidence to your woman? Do you feel the need to associate yourself with the "in" crowd? Are you comfortable in your own skin?

You are going to acquire more confidence as you become more familiar with the Lord. The strength you need to succeed in every area of your life is in Him. This concept is what many of us need to learn. Everything we are lacking or need is in God. He will not withhold His gifts from you if you do what is right according to His standards. "For the Lord God is our sun and our shield. He gives us grace and glory. The Lord will withhold no good thing from those who do what is right." {Psalm 84:11NLT}.

The confidence that I now have is a gift from the Lord. I obtained this gift as I began to understand Him more intimately. I discovered who I am as I discovered who God is. Our identity is wrapped up in Him. He does not see you from your past or even from your current state. He sees you from your future condition. Your future is as bright as the morning sun. Keep pressing. You are evolving by the day.

Here is a confession for you to pray: I am a man of excellence, and I excel in all that I do. I think big, and I get big results because I serve a big God. I go the extra mile with joy to honor God and my woman. I am a man of high standards just like Joseph, and I will maintain my standards no matter the circumstances. I am an overcomer; therefore, I succeed in all that I do. Thank You, Father, for helping me with this transformation. I am a real man, and I will demonstrate this stance daily, in Jesus' name. Amen.

See if you remember what you read in this chapter.

A real man attaches himself to

_____ _____ _____ _____ _____ _____ _____ _____ _____ things.

A Real Man Has No Fear

Matthew 1:20 But as he was thinking this over, behold, an angel of the Lord appeared to him in a dream, saying, Joseph, descendant of David, **<u>do not be afraid</u>** to take Mary {as} your wife, for that which is conceived in her is of {from, out of} the Holy Spirit {Amplified Bible}.

A real man has no fear because he walks in perfect love. "There is no fear in love; but perfect love casts out fear, because fear involves torment. But he who fears has not been made perfect in love" {1st John 4:18NKJV}. Joseph was not a fearful man. He was a loving man. The anxieties attached to the circumstances of Mary's pregnancy had no influence on his decision. He was empowered by love. Mary would have been treated completely different if the fears had swayed him. This story demonstrates the power of loving God's way.

Fear is the opposite of love. If fear is present, love is absent, and if love is absent, God is nonexistent for "God is love." Keep Him in the core of your soul by responding with love instead of fear. "He who does not love does not know God, for God is love" {1st John 4:8NKJV}.

Fear robs you of so much. Fear is the factory where all harmful emotions are manufactured. Fear is the assembly line of negative actions, attitudes, and thoughts. If Joseph had been fearful, he would have silenced the voice of the Lord and empowered the voice of Satan. A real man is the master of his feelings. It is very difficult to solve problems if you are fearful. Fear robs you of your peace and joy, and you should never make any decisions from a fearful, frustrated, or sad place. Have you ever made a fearful decision? What was the result of the fearful decision? What would have changed if you had made a loving decision instead? Engage in love rather than reaching for the hand of fear.

Love is light, and fear is darkness. Love is wisdom, and fear is ignorance. Love is humility, and fear is pride. Love listens, and fear screams. Love is calmness while fear is unrest. Love is the restorer, but fear is the thief. Love gives while fear is selfish. Love evens everything out, and fear gets even. Love forgives, and fear wallows in the hurts and pains. Love is freedom, but fear is captivity. Love embraces the truth, and fear cannot handle the truth. Love never fails, and fear always fails. Love is the end of sin, and fear is the beginning of sin. God hates {not a choice He desires for us} fear, and Satan hates love.

We see in the Bible how much the Creator hates fear: "But as for the cowards and the ignoble and the contemptible and the cravenly lacking in courage and the cowardly submissive, and as for the unbelieving and faithless, and as for the depraved and defiled with abominations, and as for murderers and the lewd and adulterous and the practicers of magic arts and the idolaters {those who give supreme devotion to anyone or anything other than God} and all liars {those who knowingly convey untruth by word or deed}—{all of these shall have} their part in the lake that blazes with fire and brimstone. This is the second death" {Revelation 21:8AMP}. Notice how the Scripture shows us that the first who are tossed into the lake of fire are the "cowards."

Fear robs you of your identity. Adam and Eve lost their identity after they disobeyed the Lord God in the Garden of Eden. Adam boldly walked with the Lord God, and he named all of the animals. However, his disobedience caused him to hide from the Lord God out of fear. "And they heard the sound of the Lord God walking in the garden in the cool of the day, and Adam and his wife hid themselves from the presence of the Lord God among the trees of the garden. But the Lord God called to Adam and said to him, where are you? He said, I heard the sound of You {walking} in the garden, and I was afraid because I was naked; and I hid myself" {Genesis 3:8-10AMP}. Fear changed the association that Adam had with the Lord God. Before Adam sinned, the connection between Adam and the Lord God was based on love but once fear entered into the equation, it caused separation between the Lord God and man.

While Adam operated out of love, he and the Lord God had all beliefs in common. However, the moment that fear entered into their relationship, Adam had a quality that the Lord God did not have. This sinful quality caused the division in their union. Therefore, fear gave Satan the legal right to enter into an alliance with Adam. This interference introduced a different way of acting, feeling, and thinking. "The wicked flee when no man pursues them, but the {uncompromisingly} righteous are bold as a lion" {Proverbs 28:1AMP}. What type of impact would fear have on you and your lady? If fear separated God and man, it will definitely separate man and woman. Fear destroys all of the ingredients needed for a successful relationship. Fear robs you of your confidence. Fear is a hindrance.

David would not have become King David if he had been fearful. One of his greatest strengths was his courage. His courage placed him head and shoulders above everyone else. His bravery led him to face Goliath, a giant of a man, and win in battle. There is always a reward for a courageous person who is inspired by God. "And the women responded as they laughed and frolicked, saying, Saul has slain his thousands, and David his ten thousands" {1st Samuel 18:7AMP}. Be determined to face life and all that it will offer, and you will win just like David did. The Lord is on your side. A real man knows the Creator is on his side. "What then shall we say to {all} this? If God is for us, who {can be} against us? {Who can be our foe, if God is on our side?}" {Romans 8:31AMP}. "He Who lives in you is greater {mightier} than he who is in the world" {1st John 4:4AMP}.

We see fearful men daily: the ones who are easily moved by their emotions, the ones who are abusive to their woman, the ones who act out of ignorance, and the ones who are selfish and prideful. Fear resides in a person's soul. I dealt with choosing fear for many years as shown through displays of uncontrollable anger. As stated earlier, I attended anger management classes several times, read numerous books, and tried meditation, but nothing I attempted worked. Actually, these efforts added to my frustrations. When everything else failed, my Heavenly Father worked. He is the only one who is capable of keeping me on the right path, and He is the one who is capable of keeping you on the right path.

Fear introduces torment as well. A person who feels the need to be constantly in control faces torment. Consider the strength and confidence that a dictator displays while he believes he is in control. Now, think about the weaknesses, actions, and lack of confidence the dictator displays the second that he knows he is no longer in control. Fear is the ruling force in the heart of his strength or weakness.

Many men are oppressors who try to have control over their woman. A dictator is not what a real man looks like. A real man acts out of love. Love is the foundation of true manhood. Remember, a real man makes the best decisions for everyone involved. Positive choices are made when love is the basis of your options. Joseph displayed love and not fear. His demonstration of love pleased God so much that God visited Joseph in a dream. Are you pleasing to the Lord? Has the Creator ever visited you while you were asleep?

Ladies, are you confident or fearful? If you are afraid, what is causing the distress? You cannot be yourself or who the Creator created you to be if you are in this negative space. Fear strips you of your identity and imprisons you. You are a woman who possesses strength; therefore, be bold and determined to conquer all fears. One of the ways to defeat fear is by simply talking about it. Usually if we are afraid of something or someone, we seal our lips and lock others out. This decision hands the keys to the warden {fear}. Share your fears with God and your man.

You are not a victim so refuse to be one. You are not a prisoner. Implement your escape plan now by exposing anyone who is victimizing you. You get your freedom by revealing the crime or criminal. Criminals are empowered not because they are bigger, smarter, or stronger than the victim but by the phobia of the prey. The abuse continues since the target is afraid to tell. The manipulation stops once the person exposes the abuser. You must hate {not a choice you desire for yourself} the mistreatment and want the pain to stop.

Exposure is the truth, and darkness is the lie. Many of us are choosing to live in the darkness {the lie} instead of exposing the fears {the truth}. Darkness does not support your relationship. If you are living in the darkness, step out of the shadow by telling, "The truth, the whole truth and nothing but the truth so help you God." Fear presents itself as a giant in many cases; however, it does fall when we confront it as David confronted the giant Goliath.

I had some fears that I had to confront. They were robbing me of a productive life. Once I tackled them, I felt like a thousand pounds were lifted off of me. Fear has no place in my life, and it should have no place in your life. You do not have a life if fear is controlling you. I transitioned from a victim to victor the minute I told my wife about the fears that were troubling me. At that point,

I had a partner fighting with me. She helped me to regain my confidence. Open your mouth, and let the light of God shine on the gloom.

Ladies, your man is the first person with whom you should speak if you are fearful. Believe it or not, any bondage that you may be experiencing also impacts him. You both are a team. This conversation informs him about the situation, and now, he can step in and assist you. Sharing your fears with him helps with his transition to becoming a real man. Every trial he goes through and passes is helping him to accept responsibility for you, the children, and himself. You need to first acknowledge fear in order to overcome it. You were created to live a victorious life, and fear prohibits you from living this life. You need to deal with all fears today and not extend the agony any longer. You will defeat all fears the moment that you are able to love like God. Read 1st Corinthians Chapter 13 to discover God's kind of love.

Fear and torment is also introduced into our lives when we have forgiveness issues. If someone has wronged you, forgive them as soon as possible. I forgave my father for not being an active part of my life. I would not be who I am today if this issue had remained alive. I love and honor my father despite the hurt and pain of his absence. Forgiveness permits us to live in the present instead of dying in the hurtful past. If we do not move forward in life, we will become stagnant and eventually die. Forgiveness is "THE" way to release yourself and the person who has wronged you.

Like a rubber band, I want to stretch you to your greater heights. Even if you are not at fault, you must confess your sins to God for not forgiving the person or people who hurt you. "If we confess our sins, he is faithful and just and will forgive us our sins and purify us from all unrighteousness" {1st John 1:9NIV}. I know this can be challenging; however, it **"MUST"** be done. You will not be able to move on in life without this courageous act. The truth is forgiveness is not for the person who has wronged you as much as it is for you. It is medicine for the soul. Will you receive it?

Pray this prayer if you are dealing with forgiveness issues. Father, I confess my sins for not forgiving _____. I repent for blocking You out of this part of my life. I am now giving You access to the darkness in my soul. Please shine Your light on my soul and the issue. Set me free from it. I forgive _____. I am no longer holding him or her or myself in bondage. I pray that the freedom which I am experiencing at this moment is also felt by _____. Fill me and _____ with Your love, in Jesus' name. Amen.

Earth is life's classroom. Are you ready for the next phase? Are you ready to graduate and completely walk into your deliverance? Every trial is an opportunity for growth and ultimately for graduation. Contact the person who has hurt you. Ask the individual to forgive you for holding him or her hostage to the sinful act. I know this is very difficult, but it can be done. I have done it. You can contact the individual by phone, letter, email, or in person. As long as we are alive, there will be a person who we **"MUST"** forgive. Jesus said, "For if you forgive men their trespasses, your heavenly Father will also forgive you. But if you do not forgive men their trespasses, neither will your Father forgive your trespasses" {Matthew 6:14-15NKJV}.

Here is a prayer for you: Father, remove any and all fears that "Roberto" and I have. I am asking You to fill us both with Your courage, determination, and love. Make Your valuable instructions plain to us during our trials, and let Your light shine through all darkness. I am so grateful that we can rely on You to help us with the issue of fear. Help us with the issue of forgiveness as well. Mend our hearts from all hurts and pains, in Jesus' name. Amen.

Reflection

Please take the time to journal your questions and comments as a powerful way to track your progress. These moments are when you take the time to reflect on what you have learned in this chapter and express your thoughts. What did you learn from this chapter? Who or what do you fear? What was the incident that introduced the fear? What impact does the fear have on your relationship? What do you need to do to get over the fear? Are you easily offended? Are you dealing with forgiveness issues? Is there someone who you have not forgiving? Do you expect for someone to forgive you if you have hurt them? Is your woman and children impacted by your inability to forgive? If so, what are you going to do to free everyone?

Here is a confession for you to pray: I am a man of excellence, and I excel in all that I do. I think big, and I get big results because I serve a big God. I go the extra mile with joy to honor God and my woman. I am a man of high standards just like Joseph, and I will maintain my standards no matter the circumstances. I am an overcomer; therefore, I succeed in all that I do. Thank You, Father, for helping me with this transformation. I am a real man, and I will demonstrate this stance daily, in Jesus' name. Amen.

See if you remember what you read in this chapter. What removes all fears?

____ ____ ____ ____ ____ ____ ____

____ ____ ____ ____.

A Real Man Values What Most People Do Not Value

Matthew 1:20 But as he was thinking this over, behold, an angel of the Lord appeared to him in a dream, saying, Joseph, descendant of David, do not be afraid **to take Mary {as} your wife**, for that which is conceived in her is of {from, out of} the Holy Spirit {Amplified Bible}.

A real man values what most people do not value. "Take Mary {as} your wife." This statement speaks volumes and truly shows us what a real man looks like. Joseph saw treasure {value} where the people of his time saw trash {something of no value at all}. God instructed Joseph to "take Mary {as} your wife," and he did. Any other man during those days would have had Mary stoned to death. So many men have killed their relationships and thrown them away. They allowed others to put a value on their relationships instead of the Creator. God sees treasure in places where people see trash. Have you thrown a valuable companionship away? Why did you view it as worthless? Were you influenced by the thoughts of others?

A real man sees beyond the surface and looks deep within the hearts of others. Beyond the surface is where we find true worth. We should not rely on exterior assessments. Conditions can appear to be one way and end up totally different. Quite a few men have missed out on a decent relationship because they were not ready to do what Joseph did. These men put no importance in their woman. They relied on the influences of the wrong people. I know some men who appreciate their car more than their lady. They realized her value after she decided to leave due to their neglect. You will always lose what you do not protect and respect.

When I first dated my wife, individuals told me that she had little value. They told me she was conceited, but I discovered the truth that she is priceless. She is the total opposite of what I was advised. I would have missed out on this treasure if I had listened to the opinions of those individuals. Strangely enough, they never really knew my wife. She has a heart made of pure gold. I am grateful that I followed Joseph's example and listened to God concerning her. My marriage is the second most valuable bond that I ever discovered. My first most prized connection is the relationship that I have with Jesus. He utilized her to change me and make me a better person. She led me to a relationship with Him. I was introduced to Jesus in the center of her living room floor some years ago. The companionship I have with her transformed me. Honestly, I do not believe I would be where I am today if I had not continued this relationship.

Let me explain that the closer I got to my wife, the more my commitment increased for God. As I learned more about her, I understood more about Him. When I comprehended how to truly love her, I knew then how to genuinely love Him. He hid this treasure in her for me to discover. When I began to search for her hidden gem, my life began to change. As I pursued her heart, I discovered the Person {Jesus} who was occupying that space, and He transformed me. He strategically utilized this vessel to teach me how to become a real man. I did not have the example of a strong father. Therefore, when I met my wife, I was a total mess. As I began to fall deeper and deeper in love with her, the Father began to clean me up. It is amazing how the Lord used a woman to teach me about true manhood. You are not going to accomplish this conversion by yourself. How else would you know you have achieved these principles? There has to be a test. Your woman is your exam and assistant all at the same time.

I would like to take this moment to thank my wife for being obedient and patient. I am so glad she did not give up on me. I was not the best person. I did not deserve her love. I am thankful that she saw the value in me even though I displayed worthlessness. I am amazed how she dealt with all of my mess and still detected a pearl. I do not know too many people who would have stuck around that long to locate it. She told me, "I saw your heart in spite of everything. I knew you were a good guy. I loved your heart." She really had to do some serious digging in order to unearth my heart. It was covered with lots of dirt from all of the hurt and pain that I had experienced. For this reason, I work overtime daily to become a real and better man.

God sees treasure in places where people see trash. I appreciate this statement so much as it shows the love that God has for us all. He does not count you out because of your economic status, education level, or past faults. The Lord loves the underdog. He cleans up dirty objects like no one else can. Anytime a man accepts what most people reject, it pleases the Creator. God is concerned about everything and everyone. He has stocks in all of us. We are priceless in His eyes. You must have the heart of the Creator in order to see and value the true worth in people. A man with God's vision is what a real man looks like. Have a heartfelt conversation with your woman, tell her how valuable she is to you, let her know how much you adore her, and apologize for your past faults. I sincerely apologized to my wife for my past faults, and she thanked me for the sincere apology. We were both liberated. It felt like we were starting all over again. This conversation can be the beginning of a new life for you both as it was for us.

Ladies, do you see the treasure in your relationship? Are you seeing value in a place where there is none? While I encourage you to look for the good in your man, be aware that some men do not have a decent heart at this point in their lives. So many women are in a relationship of no worth. They are emotionally, mentally, and spiritually bankrupted because they continue to make excuses for their man's inconsideration. You should not be in a place where you are not appreciated. You must be honest with yourself and view matters the way they really are. "It is what it is." A zebra is not a horse, and a horse is not a zebra. Although, they have similar characteristics, ultimately, they are not the same.

There is treasure in your relationship if you know your man has a sincere heart and willingness to change. The key word here is "know." I encourage you to listen to your heart. Your heart sees what your eyes cannot see. Your heart knows what your mind does not know. You know there is value in your relationship when he begins to speak and act differently and accepts responsibility for his actions. Do you feel free around him? Are you able to express yourself without any fear? Are you confident in his presence? Does he treat you like a queen? Does he respect you? If your answer is yes, then there is value in your relationship.

Appreciation is motivation. It encourages continuous change. Show your man how much you appreciate him. Let him know how much you value his efforts. I pursued change even more once my wife showed me how much she appreciated me and my efforts. I wanted all she had to offer me. A word of advice is to provide your man with what he enjoys the most. Does he like hats, ties, a nice meal, a nice card, a great big hug, or a kiss? People have a reward system in place for their children when they behave well. We are all kids at heart. Cleverly tap into your man's heart. As always, your actions advance you as well. As you help him with his transformation, it motivates you both. Certain treasures are discovered after people stretch themselves further than normal. These discoveries require more of your heart; therefore, they are the most valuable.

Do you see the value in yourself? You are a gem in spite of what you may have encountered. The Lord saw great worth in Mary, and He sees great worth in you. It is the reason He sent Jesus to die. The minute that Jesus died on the cross, your stocks flew through the roof. His act of obedience added to your treasure, and no one can take that away from you. When God created you, He constructed a one of a kind masterpiece. If you believe it, act like it. "I praise you because I am fearfully and wonderfully made; your works are wonderful, I know that full well" {Psalm 139:14NIV}. Contemplate the idea that the cross is an addition symbol {+}. It is also a multiplication symbol {x} when you tilt it. Both signs add value to any equation. Jesus + you = more than you can imagine. Jesus x you = more than you can imagine. You are priceless in the eyes of the Creator.

Here is a prayer for you: Father, thank You for opening my eyes and helping me to see the true treasure in "Jamal." Thank You for opening "Jamal's" eyes and helping him to see the true treasure in me. Father, perfect our vision. Help us to see people and situations as You see them. I am thankful that we see treasure in places where people see trash. Thank You for perfecting our golden hearts, in Jesus' name. Amen.

Reflection

Please take the time to journal your questions and comments as a powerful way to track your progress. These moments are when you take the time to reflect on what you have learned in this chapter and express your thoughts. What did you learn from this chapter? Do you truly value the relationship that you have with God, your lady, and your children? How do you protect these relationships? How do you demonstrate how much you value these relationships? Who or what have you been neglecting that requires more of your attention? Do you see value in yourself? Do you need to contact someone and apologize for making them feel worthless?

Here is a confession for you to pray: I am a man of excellence, and I excel in all that I do. I think big, and I get big results because I serve a big God. I go the extra mile with joy to honor God and my woman. I am a man of high standards just like Joseph, and I will maintain my standards no matter the circumstances. I am an overcomer; therefore, I succeed in all that I do. Thank You, Father, for helping me with this transformation. I am a real man, and I will demonstrate this stance daily, in Jesus' name. Amen.

See if you remember what you read in this chapter.

Where has God hidden our treasure?

_____ _____ _____ _____ _____.

A Real Man Is Responsible

Matthew 1:20 But as he was thinking this over, behold, an angel of the Lord appeared to him in a dream, saying, Joseph, descendant of David, do not be afraid to take Mary {as} your wife, **for that which is conceived in her is of {from, out of} the Holy Spirit** {Amplified Bible}.

A real man is a responsible man. Joseph was dealing with so much confusion regarding Mary's pregnancy, and still, God trusted him to take her as his wife. It was a package deal. His responsibility was also to the child who he did not father. Accepting responsibility has a way of molding a man into a real man.

I do not know too many men who would have done what Joseph did. He had to die to his feelings and selfish thoughts in order for Mary to live and God's purpose to be fulfilled. Most men in this situation would have played the victim role and the blame game. What responsibilities have you aborted because you played the victim role and the blame game? Accepting responsibility is a true test to becoming a real man, and it cannot be avoided. If Joseph was tested in this area, you will also be tested in this area. A real man does what most men would not do. A real man does not function based on his feelings. He functions based on the Lord's instructions.

Transforming into a real man is not easy; however, it is well worth the journey. Strenuous circumstances are no different than lifting weights. Visible weights strengthen you physically. Invisible weights strengthen you emotionally, mentally, and spiritually. Does it make sense to have a nice physique and be out of shape emotionally, mentally, and spiritually? The lack of spiritual stamina is the reason why many of us are unbalanced today. We are strong in one area of our lives and neglect the other areas. Challenges are here to shape and mold you. Again, the way you view obstacles determines how and when you come out of a difficult situation.

If you view obstacles negatively, then expect negative results. If you view obstacles as an opportunity for promotion, then expect amazing results {victory}. Have you ever heard the saying, "Whatever does not kill you will only make you stronger?" Joseph was trusted with the responsibility of protecting Mary and Jesus. He was assigned to the most precious gift given to mankind – Jesus. He could not have played the victim role and the blame game and acted responsibly. In order to be responsible, you must let go of yourself for the purpose of embracing God's plan. So many men have missed out on a beautiful relationship. They firmly hugged their outer feelings and chose not to firmly hug their woman's heart.

People will do things we do not like, and people will treat us unfairly at times. These situations do not give us the right to do to them what they have done to us. You are no different than them if you chose to repeat the senseless cycle. Repeating the senseless cycle makes you a victim and eventually a contestant in the blame game. Remember that your response is your responsibility.

In order to become a responsible man, you must accept the truth. There is freedom in the truth, "And you will know the Truth, and the Truth will set you free" {John 8:32AMP}. A real man understands the truth that he is accountable for himself only. You cannot control what others do or say; however, you can control what you do and what you say. No one should have the power to dictate what you do, how you do it, and what you say. Your responsibility is to God, yourself, your woman, and your children.

If you are not good to yourself, you will not be good to your special relationships. Dependability is what a real man looks like.

So many men believe in negotiating their responsibilities. You should not negotiate your responsibilities, but accept them and "Be All You Can Be." Joseph did not negotiate with God. He obeyed God's instructions. The Lord did not ask Joseph what he thought. God told him what to do. Joseph did not tell the Creator, "I'll do this if Mary does that. I cannot do this because Mary did that." Joseph's feelings did not outweigh the truth that his family needed him. A real man lives up to his obligations and is obedient to God's commands.

You are the protector of your family. Therefore, demonstrate protection in every aspect of their lives. They are going to honor, treasure, and admire you for your stance. They understand the amount of responsibility it takes to lead. Being a responsible man is going to require a lot of you. "For everyone to whom much is given, of him shall much be required; and of him to whom men entrust much, they will require and demand all the more" {Luke 12:48AMP}.

Great responsibilities are accompanied by challenges and rewards. Focus on the mission and not the challenges. If you are not acting responsibly in your household, you will not be responsible for anyone or anything outside of your household. "For if a man does not know how to rule his own household, how is he to take care of the church of God?" {1st Timothy 3:5NIV}.

Jesus said, "His master said to him, well done, you upright {honorable, admirable} and faithful servant! You have been faithful and trustworthy over a little; I will put you in charge of much. Enter into and share the joy {the delight, the blessedness} which your master enjoys" {Matthew 25:21AMP}. I was not always a trustworthy person. My selfish ways from the past robbed me of my responsibilities. My decision to please myself and not my wife pushed us further apart. My selfishness also impacted our children. The constant tension that I brought into our home tampered with their security. Now, I am a different man from the inside out. I am responsible for what God has entrusted to me. Are you responsible for what God has entrusted to you? The Lord has so much more for you; however, He will not give anything to anyone who is not ready for it. Are you ready for what God has for you?

I cannot imagine living my life without my wife and children. I show the Lord how much my family means to me by accepting the duties which are before me. I can handle whatever comes my way. "His divine power has given us everything we need for life and godliness through our knowledge of him who called us by his own glory and goodness" {2nd Peter 1:3NIV}.

My attitude displays to my wife and children my willingness to be responsible. The way I view myself helps me to embrace all of my responsibilities. I am a servant. I am here to serve my wife and children in every area of their lives. It takes a real man to view himself as a servant. Jesus said, "For even the Son of Man came not to have service rendered to Him, but to serve, and to give His life as a ransom for {instead of} many" {Mark 10:45AMP}.

A man who lives with a servant's mentality will never be imprisoned to anything or anyone. He is as free as a bird. This approach keeps anger, doubt, and selfishness behind the fearful bars. This mindset focuses strictly on your obligations. A real man lives a life of service. His focus is not to be served but to serve others. Responsibility is maturity on display. Jesus said, "Not so with you. Instead, whoever wants to become great among you must be your servant, and whoever wants to be first must be slave of all" {Mark 10:43-44NIV}. You are considered great by the Lord if you have a servant's mentality. If He views you as great, your lady will also. Who are you likely to tip – a waiter who gave you great service or a waiter who did not give you great service? It sure does pay to be servant minded.

Ladies, do you have a problem with serving? I have counseled quite a few women who feel challenged when it comes to ministering to their man. They feel like this position is a place of vulnerability and that it is a disadvantage. Although this belief may be valid in some cases, you should still serve your man as if you are serving God Himself. Maintain your honor. Do not let anyone get in the way of you doing the right thing. This acceptance does not mean you let him take advantage of you. This choice means you are following God's wishes. Your man cannot take advantage of you if you are doing what the Lord expects you to do. The Creator does not want you to be a fool; however, He does count on you being sensible even if your man is not being sensible. Remember, there is nothing like a true example of how to treat others. Good always wins over evil. Fulfilling God's commands is the only thing that really matters.

My wife never relinquished her duties concerning me. Her actions spoke to me even when she did not say a word. You can say anything, but can you demonstrate what you are saying? We both knew I did not deserve her thoughtfulness. Regardless, she accepted her commitment with a smile on her face. In her mind, she was not serving me, but she was serving God. There were many days that her actions stopped me in my tracks and had me reflecting on my foolish ways. I felt like a total fool. I was very disappointed in myself. I wanted to change even more because she was carrying out her responsibilities with such honor and dignity. Looking back on those times, I was a student. The Lord constantly taught me valuable lessons through her. I am still a student to this very day. He continues to teach me via Katrina. He will utilize you to do the same for your man. These life changing lessons will be taught to your man once you follow the Creator's plan. These lessons are going to make you a better person as well. Exposure to integrity teaches and equips us with added understanding. Once I learned "What Does A Real MAN Look Like," I compared him to my former self, and I developed an attraction for the qualities of a real man. My improvements are so evident that the people who knew my previous life questioned my transformation. I have one answer for them – Jesus. I am overtaken with gladness. God used my wife and the responsibilities she embraced to touch my heart and to point me in the right direction. Bless His Name!

Here is a prayer for you: Father, teach "Samuel" and I how to be more responsible with our decisions and actions. It is our desire to gain more of Your trust. We want to please You. We are going to take our focus off of us and put the focus on You. Bless us with a burning desire to satisfy You by being more responsible. I thank You that we are not moved by how we feel. Like Joseph, we are moved by Your command. I thank You for teaching us the real meaning of responsibility. We accept all of the obligations that You have for us. We are making room for more of Your responsibilities, in Jesus' name. Amen.

Reflection

Please take the time to journal your questions and comments as a powerful way to track your progress. These moments are when you take the time to reflect on what you have learned in this chapter and express your thoughts. What did you learn from this chapter? Are you a responsible person? Has God trusted you with someone or something that requires a lot of your attention and time? If so, who or what is it? How are you going to let your woman know that you are being responsible? What do you need to do to make God, your woman, and children your main focus? How much time are you investing in your household? Your household is your first responsibility. Diligently work to improve your home daily. There will be a struggle to maintain order in your life if you are lacking order in your home. What are you giving your woman when you are being responsible? SECURITY!

Here is a confession for you to pray: I am a man of excellence, and I excel in all that I do. I think big, and I get big results because I serve a big God. I go the extra mile with joy to honor God and my woman. I am a man of high standards just like Joseph, and I will maintain my standards no matter the circumstances. I am an overcomer; therefore, I succeed in all that I do. Thank You, Father, for helping me with this transformation. I am a real man, and I will demonstrate this stance daily, in Jesus' name. Amen.

See if you remember what you read in this chapter.

What did I compare strenuous circumstances to?

_____ _____ _____ _____ _____ _____ _____

_____ _____ _____ _____ _____ _____ _____.

A Real Man Is Not Prideful

Matthew 1:21 **She will bear a Son, and you shall call His name Jesus** {the Greek form of the Hebrew Joshua, which means Savior}, for He will save His people from their sins {that is, prevent them from failing and missing the true end and scope of life, which is God} {Amplified Bible}.

A real man is not a prideful man, but rather he is humble. Joseph was a humble man. He displayed humility throughout this amazing story. If he had been prideful, their outcome would have been totally different. The focus would have been on him and not on Mary's well-being. It requires a strong will to direct your attention to someone else's interests and not your own. This is what a real man looks like and does. Empathy is the ingredient many men are missing. There is a disconnection from God and your woman once this quality is lost.

This statement shows how humble Joseph really was, as he is told, "She will bear a Son, and you shall call His name Jesus." Mary is pregnant with a child who Joseph did not father. Now, he is told he cannot name the baby because the unborn child already has a name. This instruction was a test that a prideful man would not pass. Joseph passed this exam with flying colors. Humility accepts what pride rejects. During these times, it was the norm for the man to name his son and for the son to have the same name as his father or another family member. This command to name the baby "Jesus" is what you call "adding insult to injury," and yet, Joseph obeyed the Creator.

You must maintain humility because pride gets in the way of the Lord's instructions. Pride almost cost me my marriage. I had a problem admitting when I was wrong and apologizing. My ego worsened situations that were containable and made them uncontainable. Pride pushed me further away from God and my wife at one of the lowest times of my life.

Because of my prideful ways, I displayed a tough image which commanded my constant attention. I was emotionally, mentally, and spiritually fatigued, and as a result, my marriage was on its last leg. Pride is a terrible emotion that is never alone. Imagine fighting for countless rounds and being hit with punches of fear, anger, hate, and low self-esteem, etc. Do you feel your relationship can mature with this harmful emotion in the center of it?

A prideful man does not hurt in one area of his life. He hurts in every area of his life. Pride is so vicious that it snowballs into the lives of other people. It is a damaging force. It must be eliminated if you want to experience a healthy relationship. You eliminate it through humility. Scripture is clear regarding the issue of pride, "God opposes the proud but favors the humble" {James 4:6NLT}. If God opposes pride, your woman will certainly oppose pride. Pride is a dirty vehicle that becomes clean after it goes through the car wash {humility}. Pride is fear. A prideful man is really a fearful man. You know the destructive impact that fear will have on your relationship. A real man is not prideful or fearful. A real man is meek. Meekness is a different state of mind. Meekness and ego cannot dwell in the same place just as fresh water and salt water cannot flow from the same spring. "Can both fresh water and salt water flow from the same spring? My brothers, can a fig tree bear olives, or a grapevine bear figs? Neither can a salt spring produce fresh water" {James 3:11-12NIV}.

Humility is like exercising. It improves your overall health and mentality. A humble man operates under different principles than that of a prideful man. A humble man owns self-control, and a prideful man disowns self-control. A humble man operates by love, and a prideful man operates by fear. A humble man is peaceful, and a prideful man is miserable. A humble man is not moved by his emotions, and a prideful man is ruled by his emotions. A humble man is trustworthy, and a prideful man cannot be trusted. A humble man displays strength, and a prideful man displays weakness. A humble man presses on, and a prideful man gives up. A humble man endures to the end, and a prideful man quits easily. A humble man operates by faith, and a prideful man operates by his senses.

A humble man delivers the sunshine while a prideful man produces the clouds. Your woman is a flower. She needs the sunshine in order to grow but does not need the storms. Every downpour you create pushes her further away from you. You are to bring her calmness and happiness rather than discord and misery. You are to add to her life in a positive way. Humility is essential. A humble man supplies a healthy environment by yielding to God's will. Can a flower blossom in a drenching environment?

Men often move from one extreme to another in handling their ego. If you wrestle with humility, work slowly to become more modest. Humility is not an act. Humility is a lifestyle. It is not something you force, but rather it should be as natural as a fish swimming in the water. It is better to let life operate by an accepted flow instead of by force. A real man does not operate by pushing or shoving but by a pleasant tide. As a wise philosopher once said, "Don't push the river. It flows by itself."

Humility does not mean you talk low, hold your head down, or present yourself as a weak individual. If these are your thoughts, you really need to seek God for clarity. A humble man has far more strength than a prideful man. A humble man is strong in his identity and spirit while a prideful man is weak in his identity and spirit. More strength is required to live by your spirit than by your flesh {your emotions}. Your spirit has to be the driving force in your life in order for you to succeed. This truth is what Joseph knew and why he was a real man. "Then he said to me, this is what the Lord says to Zerubbabel: It is not by force nor by strength, but by my Spirit, says the Lord of Heaven's Armies" {Zechariah 4:6NLT}. I define the word humility by saying it is a mixture of self-control and steady confidence. This combination is very attractive. It is a reassuring attribute which soothes the spirit and soul of others. These are the words associated with a humble man: love, joy, peace, patience, kindness, goodness, faithfulness, gentleness, and self-control {Galatians 5:22-23NIV}. These nine characteristics are known as "The Fruit of The Spirit."

A real man displays these nine characteristics. Therefore, everyone he meets is able to partake of these fruits. Imagine having the ability to feed the world. Imagine having the ability to put an end to world hunger {spiritual famine}. When you are a manufacturer of these fruits, you can meet a person who is hungry for love and supply that need. You can meet a person who is starving for patience and provide that necessity. No one will ever leave you feeling hungry once these fruits are a part of your nature. This way of living is accomplished by the Spirit of God. Again, the common truth is God. He has to be your source and foundation to become a real man. He is the reason why I learned this information, and now, I am able to share it with you. Thank You, Jesus!

Be realistic and patient with yourself. You did not become prideful overnight, and you will not develop humility while you are sleeping. "Rome was not built in a day; however, it was built." Once this construction is completed, you, your woman, and children are going to experience life as the Grand Architect designed for it to be.

148

Ladies, if you want your man to transform into the man who I am describing, you need not to be prideful. Do not let negativity linger in your relationship. Quickly free yourself and your man of all negative feelings. Pride needs negativity so it can live. For this reason, I am asking you to display humility. Remain where the light is, and eventually he is going to see it. If pride is around and refuses to leave, apologize. Yes, apologize, even if you are not at fault. Change your attitude. In this case, you are not admitting to any guilt. I am asking you to say, "I am sorry" because your actions weakens his prideful ways. Your actions will open his heart, and your light will remove the darkness. "You are the light of the world—like a city on a hilltop that cannot be hidden. No one lights a lamp and then puts it under a basket. Instead, a lamp is placed on a stand, where it gives light to everyone in the house. In the same way, let your good deeds shine out for all to see, so that everyone will praise your heavenly Father" {Matthew 5:13-16NLT}.

If your man is acting inappropriately, you say to him, "Honey, I am sorry for offending you. Please forgive me. I love you." Your man will look at you as if you are crazy, and you are crazy. You are crazy enough to love him is spite of how he is acting, and you are crazy enough to give him the opposite of what he is giving you. This approach helps him with his transformation. Someone has to make sense and if you both are acting senseless, nothing will be accomplished. Where is God in the midst of it all? You cannot be led by your ego if you want the Lord to get involved. Examine the apology. "Honey, I am sorry for offending you." Notice, I did not say, "Honey, I am sorry "if" I offended you." Stating your apology with the word "if" dims your bright light and keeps the negativity going. When you accept the responsibility to remain a humble bright light, it takes the focus off of you and keeps it on him. Let him own his foolish actions. You do not have to own them, and you should not. Your apology will feel strange to you, but it will feel very strange to him. He knows deep down on the inside that you did not do anything wrong. The power of humility is that you may feel imprisoned when it is in operation; however, the end result is freedom for everyone who is involved. This method is how you allow your light to shine in the midst of darkness. This situation should not be a battle of wills, but it should be a battle of your willingness to remain humble. God needs an entry point to get involved in your relationship. Humility is His entry point.

I have learned that the statement, "I am sorry" can be just as powerful as "I love you," if it is genuine. You must mean it once you apologize. Again, you are not expressing sorrow for any guilt. You did not do anything wrong. Think about how sincere your apology would be if this position was your focus: you are apologizing for him and his foolish actions. Can you visualize the power of this concept? These principles are challenging and life changing all at the same time. These values may seem impossible to achieve; however, we have the model in Joseph, and we have even a better model in Jesus. Ponder on the truth that while Jesus was crucified on the cross, He said, "Father, forgive them, for they don't know what they are doing" {Luke 23:34NLT}. Now, Jesus did no wrong, He was falsely accused, mistreated, and still, He prayed for them and forgave them. If Jesus could display humility during the worse event that any human being has ever suffered, you can also. Remember, you can do it. There are no excuses but only choices.

The remarkable act of humility that Jesus displayed on the cross opened the doors of Heaven. His statement, "Father, forgive them, for they don't know what they are doing" were not just random words. I believe His words pierced some of the hearts of the people who supported His crucifixion. His ability to forgive opened the doors of Heaven for the individuals who had a change of heart. Even at His worst moments, He remained humble displaying amazing spiritual strength. Pride shuts the doors of Heaven, but "Humility" unlocks them. Thank You, Jesus! Finally, pride keeps you away from the Lord, and you should not let anyone or anything keep you away from Him. Be quick to forgive just like Jesus and refuse to become a victim. People face certain destruction when pride is around. "Pride goes before destruction, a haughty spirit before a fall" {Proverbs 16:18NIV}.

Here is a prayer for you: Father, help "Walter" and I with the emotion of pride. Pride is not of You, and it has no place in us. Give us the humility needed to destroy any and all prideful ways. Show us when we are wrong. Give us the courage to apologize whenever an apology is needed. Flush pride completely out of us and fill us with the humility that Jesus displayed. Let Your light shine during our darkest moments. Let Your love be the force that directs us daily, in Jesus' name. Amen.

Reflection

Please take the time to journal your questions and comments as a powerful way to track your progress. These moments are when you take the time to reflect on what you have learned in this chapter and express your thoughts. What did you learn from this chapter? Are you a prideful person? If so, what is the source of your prideful attitude? What steps should you take from this day forward to uproot pride and embrace humility? Are you truly a believer or follower of Jesus if you refuse to forgive? Is pride in the way of you experiencing a loving relationship?

Write the word "humility" on the top of a blank piece of paper and list 12 benefits of this choice of action. Now, read what you wrote aloud daily. An example may include, "When I am humble, my wife and I are in perfect harmony" or "When I am humble, I am in God's good and perfect will."

Here is a confession for you to pray: I am a man of excellence, and I excel in all that I do. I think big, and I get big results because I serve a big God. I go the extra mile with joy to honor God and my woman. I am a man of high standards just like Joseph, and I will maintain my standards no matter the circumstances. I am an overcomer; therefore, I succeed in all that I do. Thank You, Father, for helping me with this transformation. I am a real man, and I will demonstrate this stance daily, in Jesus' name. Amen.

See if you remember what you read in this chapter.

Pride goes before what?

____ ____ ____ ____ ____ ____ ____ ____ ____ ____ ____.

A Real Man Fulfills God's Will

Matthew 1:22-23 **All this took place that it might be fulfilled** which the Lord had spoken through the prophet, 23 Behold, the virgin shall become pregnant and give birth to a Son, and they shall call His name Emmanuel—which, when translated, means, God with us {Amplified Bible}.

A real man fulfills God's will. Joseph fulfilled the Creator's will, and everyone profited from his decision. Fulfilling the Lord's will requires all of you and none of you at the same time. It demands all of you to be in agreement with God's will: emotionally, financially, mentally, physically, and spiritually, but it also needs none of your anger, doubt, disobedience, fear, or pride. I struggled with God's will for a good portion of my life. His will challenged everything that I stood for and believed. Because of my spiritual maturity, I am no longer struggling with His will. I embrace it with open arms.

It can be hard to understand God's will. There are more situations that you are not going to understand than there will be situations that you will understand. This reason is why many of us struggle with God's will. As people, we want to understand how and why the Creator allows certain things to happen. If we know everything, neither faith nor God is needed. God never intended for us to live our lives independently from Him. "The Lord our God has secrets known to no one. We are not accountable for them, but we and our children are accountable forever for all that he has revealed to us, so that we may obey all the terms of these instructions" {Deuteronomy 29:29NLT}.

The Father's will always protects His children. Because of my growth, I am no longer concerned with all of the details of life. Now, my relationship with God is based on faith not knowing how and why certain things happen. I hold onto the truth that if I take care of God's business, He will take care of my business. My decision to accept His will has given me freedom in the true sense of the word. "For My thoughts are not your thoughts, neither are your ways My ways, says the Lord. For as the heavens are higher than the earth, so are My ways higher than your ways and My thoughts than your thoughts" {Isaiah 55:8-9AMP}. I love the Bible so much because God explains to us that He has a method and a purpose for all He does. The Lord tells us we are not thinking like Him, and our ways of doing things are different than His ways of doing things. He also expresses that His system and logic are not of this world but of Heaven. Heaven represents higher principles. We must elevate our values in order to perceive life as God does.

It is the Lord's will for us to trust Him completely. We cannot fulfill His will without trust. We have to trust Him in spite of life's issues. "Trust in the Lord with all your heart and lean not on your own understanding; in all your ways acknowledge him, and he will make your paths straight" {Proverbs 3:5-6NIV}. This submission is not easy, but nothing comes easily once it has tremendous importance attached to it. You, your woman, and children are of tremendous importance to the Lord. Allow His will to come to fruition just like Joseph did.

Joseph struggled with God's will {"do not be afraid to take Mary as your wife"}. To help him, God spoke to him in his dream and revealed His plan. God knows how difficult it can be to fulfill His will. For this reason, He will comfort you during the process. His reassurance does not mean you will not experience some uneasiness; however, you must not quit but follow His instructions one step at a time. You are not alone. God was with Joseph, and He is also with you. I am speaking from experience. The process of learning to follow God's will was challenging, but I was strengthened with every step I took. It purified me and got rid of the negative thoughts I was carrying. It saved my life and marriage. It refined my reasoning and character. God never said that we will not experience challenges. God said, He will be with us and help us through the challenges. The process cannot be avoided. We must walk it out. "Even when I walk through the darkest valley, I will not be afraid, for you are close beside me. Your rod and your staff protect and comfort me" {Psalm 23:4NLT}. Truthfully, the process never stops because learning and evolving into the mind of Christ never stops. God said, "Let this same attitude and purpose and {humble} mind be in you which was in Christ Jesus: {Let Him be your example in humility}" {Philippians 2:5AMP}. I have a better understanding of the Lord's will due to my willingness to study His word. The more you are familiarized with His word, the more you will be familiarized with His voice. How can you fulfill God's will if you are not familiar with His voice? "My sheep hear My voice, and I know them, and they follow Me" {John 10:27NKJV}.

Even Jesus struggled with God's will. "Saying, Father, if You are willing, remove this cup from Me; yet not My will, but {always} Yours be done. And there appeared to Him an angel from heaven, strengthening Him in spirit. And being in an agony {of mind}, He prayed {all the} more earnestly and intently, and His sweat became like great clots of blood dropping down upon the ground" {Luke 22:42-44AMP}.

Jesus prayed for God to remove the process of crucifixion, but He also stated, "Yet not My will, but {always} Yours be done." This illustration is absolutely amazing. The battle between our wills and God's will is always at war with each other. Jesus shows us how to fight this battle and win. As stated earlier, self-talk is a vital practice which you must master. Jesus shows us whose will is of more importance by humbling Himself. Humility is the way to embrace God's will. Look at the struggle Jesus had. What kind of battle would have you sweating blood? Jesus toiled with the Creator's will so much that "His sweat became like great clots of blood dropping down upon the ground." What a great model Jesus is. He shows us that the choices of God will challenge us at times, but they are always the better options. "For we do not have a High Priest Who is unable to understand and sympathize and have a shared feeling with our weaknesses and infirmities and liability to the assaults of temptation, but One Who has been tempted in every respect as we are, yet without sinning" {Hebrews 4:15AMP}. You can petition the Father concerning His will, but understand that the final outcome is in His hands.

As Jesus struggled in the Garden of Gethsemane just before his crucifixion, God strengthened Him. God did not remove Him from the struggle, but rather He strengthened Him in the struggle. Following God's will makes us stronger and better during the testing periods of our lives. Note that Jesus was not strengthened physically, but He was strengthened spiritually. Your spirit will not be strengthened if you avoid God's will. Your spirit will not develop maturely if you dodge the process. Just as God comforted Joseph and Jesus, He will also comfort you. You are equipped and able to meet His instructions if you chose.

This scripture {Luke 22:42-44} says that Jesus was "in an agony {of mind}." God introduces His thoughts and ways to us by challenging our reasoning. Jesus understood His Father's reasoning; therefore, He was able to carry out His Father's will. What person or thing prevents you from understanding God's reasoning? We have a tendency to embrace relationships that prevent us from experiencing God's will. You must bury unhealthy relationships. Have a funeral for anything that commands your attention in a harmful way. Put damaging temptations such as pornography, drugs, alcohol, selfishness, and adultery six feet under. This is what a real man looks like and does. Trust the Lord even though you may be challenged. He will be there with you every step of the way empowering you. He will even visit you in your dreams. A real man is willing to accept all that God has to offer in order to fulfill God's will.

Ladies, the Lord has a purpose concerning your relationship. Do you know what it is? Are you pleasing your selfish feelings instead of listening to God's will? His plans and what feels good can be two different ideas. You have to seek His will daily as Jesus did. In His commands are valuable instructions which will help your man with his transformation. Discovering God's will is vital. How do you locate it? Prayer reveals what His choices are for you. Prayer is a time to intimately interact with the Lord granting Him access to your relationship. He has your permission to lead you the moment you pray.

At one time, my wife considered divorcing me. She prayed about it and waited for God's instructions. He replied, "Stay. Do not go anywhere." Surprising! If she had asked her family or friends, they would have said, "This relationship is not God's will for you. Leave him." God's response shocked her. She could not believe it. She was convinced that divorcing me was the only answer and seemed like the right thing to do. However, it was not God's will. I am so thankful for a praying woman who recognizes the Creator's voice.

Prayer delivers understanding. God will give you the answers to your questions as you pray. Prayer is a way of comprehending God's thoughts and ways. Your prayer life needs to be a top priority.

Permit the Lord's will to be satisfied even though it is not easy. There is nothing like pleasing God. You will be pleased as well. In His will, you find refuge and guidance. Once His plan is implemented, your life will improve. He has interests concerning every area of your life. He will teach you how to experience Heaven here on earth. Intensify your prayer life, and you will begin to experience this growth. I am experiencing Heaven here on earth in every area of my life. Thank You, Jesus! Understanding more about God's will has given me a new way of thinking and living. His ways and methods are just amazing.

The relationship you have with the Creator is a partnership and should be treated as such. There are certain requirements you have to meet in order for it to blossom. Play your part, and He will play His. How much effort are you putting forth to discover His purpose? Spend time with Him, and by doing so, His plan will be outlined for you. Be prepared for the unexpected. His commands will take you on quite a journey. Once you are led by His Spirit, He will aid and assist you every step of the way. Ladies, you can direct your man towards God's will by your loving attitude. Remember, you both are a team and what impacts you also impacts him.

Pray for the Father's will to be established in your life and relationship daily. Jesus taught us a specific prayer with the Lord's Prayer. I encourage you to recite this prayer everyday {Matthew 6:9-13NKJV}.

"Our Father in heaven, Hallowed be Your name. Your kingdom come. Your will be done on earth as it is in heaven. Give us this day our daily bread. And forgive us our debts, as we forgive our debtors. And do not lead us into temptation, but deliver us from the evil one. For Yours is the kingdom and the power and the glory forever. Amen."

Reflection

Please take the time to journal your questions and comments as a powerful way to track your progress. These moments are when you take the time to reflect on what you have learned in this chapter and express your thoughts. What did you learn from this chapter? How important is it for you to be in God's will? What is stopping you from fully embracing the Lord's will? Something old has to die in order for something new to live. What must die in your life so that your new nature can live? What connection is hindering you from accomplishing the Creator's will? Why are you holding onto this relationship?

Joseph thought he had two choices: B. Divorce Mary secretly C. Have her stoned to death. Neither of these choices was in God's will. If your options do not reflect the Lord's desire, it is not His will for you. Choice "A" was revealed to Joseph when the Creator spoke to him in a dream. When your thoughts and God's thoughts differ, go into a place of rest. God expressed His blueprint to Joseph and laid out His plan which was to marry Mary. At that point, the diagram of her pregnancy was made known. The truth you are seeking about any issue is framed in the Illustrator's illustration. Seek His plan daily, and your relationship will develop like never before. This is what a real man looks like and does.

Men, pray for God's will to be established in your life and relationship daily. Jesus taught us a specific prayer with the Lord's Prayer. I encourage you to recite this prayer everyday {Matthew 6:9-13NKJV}.

"Our Father in heaven, Hallowed be Your name. Your kingdom come. Your will be done on earth as it is in heaven. Give us this day our daily bread. And forgive us our debts, as we forgive our debtors. And do not lead us into temptation, but deliver us from the evil one. For Yours is the kingdom and the power and the glory forever. Amen."

Here is a confession for you to pray: I am a man of excellence, and I excel in all that I do. I think big, and I get big results because I serve a big God. I go the extra mile with joy to honor God and my woman. I am a man of high standards just like Joseph, and I will maintain my standards no matter the circumstances. I am an overcomer; therefore, I succeed in all that I do. Thank You, Father, for helping me with this transformation. I am a real man, and I will demonstrate this stance daily, in Jesus' name. Amen.

See if you remember what you read in this chapter.

What two places did God compare His ways and thoughts to?

____ ____ ____ ____ ____ ____ & ____ ____ ____ ____ ____.

A Real Man Obeys God

Matthew 1:24 Then Joseph, being aroused from his sleep, **did as the angel of the Lord had commanded him:** he took {her to his side as} his wife {Amplified Bible}.

A real man obeys God. Joseph was a real man who obeyed God. The Lord honors obedience, "But Samuel replied, what is more pleasing to the Lord: your burnt offerings and sacrifices or your obedience to his voice? Listen! Obedience is better than sacrifice, and submission is better than offering the fat of rams." {1st Samuel 15:22NLT}. The Great Architect has a plan for every one of us. His plan is His will. His plan cannot be accomplished without a submissive person. Obedience is the foundation, brick, and cement of the construction site. There is no building without it. A healthy relationship in Heaven or earth is absent without obedience. Your relationship with the Creator cannot grow past the level of your submission. He is a Gentleman. He will never force His ways on us. For this reason, He gave us all a free will. This truth is the reason why we have to invite Him into our relationship. Without our invitation, He is a spectator that stands on the outside waiting for our approval. "Here I am! I stand at the door and knock. If anyone hears my voice and opens the door, I will come in and eat with him, and he with me" {Revelation 3:20NIV}. He is the Great Architect. He is the Builder of everything. He has the key to every lock, and yet, He is knocking at the door of our heart waiting for us to answer.

There are several qualities you need to have in place in order to be obedient. First, you need to recognize the voice of the Father. You may hear three voices at any given time. The one you answer shows if you are being obedient or not. There is God's voice, your voice, and the devil's voice. The Father's voice is always escorted by His promises. His voice lines up with His word.

Obeying His voice has many benefits. It prevents us from experiencing future hurts and pains. There were times that God spoke to me, and I ignored His counsel. The results were not good. My disobedience caused my wife and me moments of separation due to senseless fights and arguments. We were physically in our home; however, we did not communicate with each other. She rested comfortably in the bed while I tossed and turned on the couch. A real man does what the Lord commands him to do. My dishonor to the Creator resulted in me dishonoring my wife. No woman appreciates dishonor. Recognizing and respecting God's voice rejects dishonor.

Secondly, you must have the discipline not to rush into what feels good. For instance, it may feel good to get even with your woman if you are angry at her, but getting even is not in God's plan. You cannot live an obedient life without self-control. Self-control sets boundaries. In the past, I have let my emotions get the best of me. The lack of self-control taught me painful lessons that I could have easily avoided. I have met and counseled countless people who were rebellious because they lacked self-control. Many of them entered the prison system. The prisons are overpopulated with men, women, boys, and girls who refused to obey the law. There are penalties in place for people who are disobedient in this world and in the spiritual world. A real man understands that his actions have consequences. Discipline is a key to living an obedient lifestyle.

Thirdly, you need to be considerate in order to be obedient. I believe Joseph showed lots of consideration for the Creator and Mary. As the Instructor told Joseph what to do, he did it. He did not complain or make excuses. Obedience is just doing what you are told to do. I believe obedience is the highest form of respect to God since it requires your total submission. Absolute surrender is an area of struggle for many people. When you are a considerate person, the struggle is eliminated.

The greatest lesson I ever learned about obedience came from my then five year old son, Antonio. At his school field day, he was paired up with a little girl, and they were both competing against each other. He was winning all of the competitions, and I sensed his partner's frustration. So, I pulled him to the side and asked him to lose the next event. Without giving it a second thought, he agreed to my request. I did not know that the following event was Tug-O-War. As soon as we arrived at the station, I felt horrible. I had directed him to lose this match to a girl when this contest clearly showed superior strength. To make matters worse, his friends were at the station watching. They both grabbed the rope, and he allowed her to beat him two out of three times. You should have seen the million dollar smile on her face. She finally won a competition and displayed her strength over a boy. The win really boosted her self-esteem. Surprising enough, Antonio was not upset by the defeat. He did not accept peer pressure from his friends. He was totally devoted to obeying my wishes. His focus was on our agreement and not his feelings. This moment is one of the greatest experiences that I have ever had, and it came at the expense of a five year old boy who was willing to obey his father's desire. My request was far from weakness. My request was a sign of absolute strength. His obedience was a blessing to everyone. His actions taught me a valuable lesson that I will never forget. I can still remember his partner's mother thanking him and me. I recall teachers and other parents describing him as a gentleman. I often think of the smiles on his face and his partner's face. They were both winners that day.

Jesus obeyed His Father, and we are all winners for His act of obedience once we believe in Him. There is power in obedience, great strength in obeying, amazing control in surrendering, life changing lessons in submitting, and the ultimate expression of love in conforming. Your woman will be drawn to your obedience and so will God. A real man obeys God no matter the situation. Thank You, Father, for allowing me to feel the way that You felt as Your Son obeyed You. For a moment in time, You allowed me to experience the pleasure of an obedient son. Thank you, Jesus!

Say this prayer whenever you need to: Father, I apologize for disobeying You. It is my desire to accomplish the plans that You have for my life. I know I please You when I obey You. I will spend more time with You so that I can become more familiar with Your voice. I thank You, Father, for hearing and granting me my request. I love You. I am going to demonstrate unwavering obedience from this day forward, in Jesus' name. Amen.

Ladies, the power of love changed my life, and the act of obedience was the evidence of true love. My wife loved me even though it was challenging. The obedience that she displayed to God was pure worship in action. Her deeds impressed me more than anything else. It took amazing control to love me, but she found strength and comfort in what she was doing. She was obeying the Lord. Never did I view her submission as weakness, but rather I viewed her submission as strength. Her respect for God commanded my attention. I admired her. The more she obeyed the Father, the more I respected her. I am still amazed at her and all that she did. As I look back, I understand that the Director was behind the scenes orchestrating her actions and my growth.

When you are obedient to God, your man will appreciate you and want to do better. Your obedience will expose his disobedience. Your honor will provoke him to change. In your loyalty to God, there are life changing lessons which He will utilize. These teachings will assist your man with his transformation. I have learned some of the most inspiring principles from my wife. Her submission to God really helped me during my transformation. If she did not submit to God, I would have missed these godly deposits. My wife and I overcame many battles together. She carried me on her back while I was discovering the road to true manhood. Her act of obedience nursed me as it displayed the unconditional love of God. You can never go wrong once you are obeying the Lord.

Here is a prayer for you: Father, give "Gary" and me a heart to obey You. Teach us how to follow You in spite of how we feel. Jesus has shown us the importance of obedience. It is my desire that "Gary" and I follow Jesus' footsteps. It is not about us, but it is all about You. I pray for the mindset that not our will but Your will be done. I thank You in advance for answering this prayer and for granting me my heart's desire, in Jesus' name. Amen.

Say this prayer whenever you need to: Father, I apologize for disobeying You. It is my desire to accomplish the plans that You have for my life. I know I please You when I obey You. I will spend more time with You so that I can become more familiar with Your voice. I thank You, Father, for hearing and granting me my request. I love You. I am going to demonstrate unwavering obedience from this day forward, in Jesus' name. Amen.

Reflection

Please take the time to journal your questions and comments as a powerful way to track your progress. These moments are when you take the time to reflect on what you have learned in this chapter and express your thoughts. What did you learn from this chapter? What is the main lesson that you have learned from being disobedient? What are the top three mistakes you made due to rebellion? Do you see the importance of submitting to God? Can you ever justify disobeying God? How do you feel when your child/children disobey you? How do you suppose the Lord feels once you disobey Him?

Here is a confession for you to pray: I am a man of excellence, and I excel in all that I do. I think big, and I get big results because I serve a big God. I go the extra mile with joy to honor God and my woman. I am a man of high standards just like Joseph, and I will maintain my standards no matter the circumstances. I am an overcomer; therefore, I succeed in all that I do. Thank You, Father, for helping me with this transformation. I am a real man, and I will demonstrate this stance daily, in Jesus' name. Amen.

See if you remember what you read in this chapter.

What is obedience the highest form of?

_____ _____ _____ _____ _____ _____ _____.

A Real Man Treats His Woman as His Equal

Matthew 1:24 Then Joseph, being aroused from his sleep, did as the angel of the Lord had commanded him: **he took {her to his side as} his wife** {Amplified Bible}.

A real man treats his woman as his equal. Joseph did not deal with Mary as if she was lesser than him. He treated her with special care and was more concerned about her than he was about himself. There is never a justifiable reason to treat a person badly. You maintain control of the situation and yourself by treating a person the way that you would like to be treated. This is what a real man looks like.

The Lord blessed the world with women. He did not intend for them to be treated as second class citizens. When God created Eve, He did not take her from Adam's back. He took her from Adam's side. When a man and a woman are standing at the altar, she stands by her soon to be husband's side. One word comes to mind as I am pondering on this truth – equality. It is safe to say that this position is the rightful place for women. Do you agree? "And the Lord God caused a deep sleep to fall upon Adam; and while he slept, He took one of his ribs or a part of his side and closed up the {place with} flesh. And the rib or part of his side which the Lord God had taken from the man He built up and made into a woman, and He brought her to the man. Then Adam said, this {creature} is now bone of my bones and flesh of my flesh; she shall be called Woman, because she was taken out of a man" {Genesis 2:21-23AMP}.

Quite a few men have failed or are failing in their relationship because they view women as the lesser creation. I once viewed women this way. My thoughts were influenced by the men I admired, television, and music. This attitude did not sit well with my wife. I can remember her always telling me, "You are not better than me. I have feelings too. I am your equal." In my mind, I pictured the image of a caveman mistreating a cavewoman as he dragged her by her hair. When I was younger, I saw a cartoon with this segment, and this ridiculous image was imprinted in my mind. Therefore, when my wife expressed her opinion or disagreed with me, I saw it as disrespect. I expected for her to remain silent just like the cavewoman. I did not see her as my equal. I did not have a good understanding of true leadership. This mentality was hard to break, and it caused lots of hurt and pain. I represented a barbarian/dictator who made my children and other family members victims. This thoughtless approach elevates your head above the clouds {ego}. To me, my feelings, opinions, and advice were of superior importance. Who wants to be around an inflated person? How can a union grow with this sort of dysfunction? Think of the letters of "ego" spelling "edging God out." If your ego is most important in your life, change your perspective. This attitude will never work in any relationship.

I was on the verge of losing my family. Remember, you will always lose what you do not protect and respect. An effective leader is moved by wisdom rather than ignorance. I applaud my wife for sticking it out with me even though it was difficult for her. I interfered with her security. For this reason, many women have left their relationship in pursuit of another one. Women easily find another man attractive when they feel neglected or belittled. For some strange reason, a man quickly realizes his woman's value when another man has her attention. Why does he realize her value then?

"And the Lord God caused a deep sleep to fall upon Adam; and while he slept, He took one of his ribs or a part of his side and closed up the {place with} flesh. And the rib or part of his side which the Lord God had taken from the man He built up and made into a woman, and He brought her to the man" {Genesis 2:21-22AMP}. The Lord God could have formed Eve the same way He formed Adam {from the dust of the ground}. "Then the Lord God formed man from the dust of the ground and breathed into his nostrils the breath or spirit of life, and man became a living being" {Genesis 2:7AMP}. He could have even spoken her into existence as He did with the other creations, but instead He built her from Adam's rib. Eve was the only creation made from a living being. Therefore, women are the carrier of life.

The main purpose of the rib cage is to protect our organs. It forms a barrier that encloses our heart and lungs. This location was the construction site of the woman. What do you think the Lord had in mind with this plan? Everything God does has a specific reason. The woman was established from protection in the very beginning. That is why we must protect our women to the very end. This idea is God's original intention for women, and it is His final decision. He is not going to change his mind.

Would you treat your heart as a lesser organ? Of course not! Neither are women lesser to men. You must protect your woman's heart. To protect your woman's heart means to handle her with special care. A man has to be skilled when it comes to handling his chosen lady. Let your woman be who she is. Do not attempt to change or mold her into who you will like for her to be. She has her own way of being, speaking, and acting just as you do. Respect her differences. As you value her, you are treating her as your equal. I understand that you may not always agree with your woman, what she says, or how she acts at times. It is your responsibility to respect your queen. This skillful approach is what Joseph did with Mary, and God mended the state of their relationship. Joseph maintained his poise and treated Mary as his equal. He took her to his side as his wife.

Would you treat your lungs as a lesser organ? Of course not! Neither are women lesser to men. You must protect your woman's lungs by allowing her the space to inhale and exhale. My wife and I know the importance of the lungs. Years ago, we experienced the painful loss of a child when our son Jeremiah was born prematurely. The cause of his death was undeveloped lungs. His heart was developed; however, his lungs needed more time. The lungs are a magnificent organ that performs a multitude of vital functions every second of our lives. Breathing is the most essential of these functions. With each breath, the lungs take in oxygen {life} and removes carbon dioxide {death}.

The movie "Waiting to Exhale" was very popular among women as the characters had the space to inhale and exhale. Although, my wife was able to inhale, I did not allow her the space to exhale. My constant criticism represented carbon dioxide; therefore, my marriage was dying. I violated and criticized my wife constantly due to my distorted views of women, and as a result, we were rapidly growing further apart.

Your woman is not lower than you. If she was of lesser value, the Creator would have called her the lesser creation. He called her a "Helper" which means she is your supporter. She will aid you in accomplishing many things in your life. "Now the Lord God said, it is not good {sufficient, satisfactory} that the man should be alone; I will make him a helper {suitable, adapted and complementary} for him" {Genesis 2:18AMP}. The Creator planned to bless Adam with two amazing gifts. God's first gift to Adam was the connection they shared, and His second gift was Eve. Eve was the gift who resulted in marriage. Marriage is the ultimate partnership that a man and a woman can share with each other.

The Lord God said, "It is not good for man to be alone," and yet, men all over the world are alone due to their twisted views of women. I know quite a few successful men who would not have succeeded without the role of their woman. I can speak from personal experience. There were times that I felt like giving up on my goals, but my wife did not allow me to quit. She picked up my abandoned goals and carried them for me when I could not carry them any longer. I owe my success to the Creator first and to my wife second. I am not afraid to admit to you that at times she was stronger than me. She is my helper and my partner. I praise the Lord for her. He knew the day would come when I would want to give up on my goals, and He also knew my wife would there to help, motivate, and inspire me along the way. Her actions were a true depiction of teamwork. Where would I be today without her constant encouragement, passion, and dedication? She is my companion, and the reason why this book is written. She is my best friend, my wife, the mother of my youngest child, and the person who helped me to produce my deepest dreams.

Men are not able to give physical life while women house, carry, and deliver life. How can we view any woman as beneath us? I have learned to truly appreciate and pay tribute to women for all that they do and endure. The Bible states, "God saved the best for last," and I agree. Women are the final physical handiwork who God produced, and His best creation fit for man. "And the master of the banquet tasted the water that had been turned into wine. He did not realize where it had come from, though the servants who had drawn the water knew. Then he called the bridegroom aside, and said, "Everyone brings out the choice wine first and then the cheaper wine after the guests have had too much to drink; but you have saved the best till now" {John 2:9-10NIV}.

How would you treat your woman if every day was Mother's Day? How do you think she would feel if she felt appreciation to this degree? Is she not worth it? If you make your woman feel good, she is going to make you feel good. The better you make her feel, the better she is going to make you feel. Feeling good is contagious. She will want to keep this great flow going. The more you give her, the more she is going to give to you. People usually say, "In relationships you are to give and take." I have a different point of view. Do not focus on taking more than focusing on giving. I believe, "In relationships you are to give and give." Give, and do not stop giving, and watch what happens. Become consumed to the point of automatically giving. The only things you should take are: burdens, frustrations, fears, and pressures and then hand them over to the Son {Jesus}. He will shine His amazing light on you and the situation.

Ladies, there is not another creation on the planet like you. God handcrafted you as a masterpiece. Carry yourself with respect and dignity in spite of what you may have faced. You have not lost any worth at all, but your value has increased because of everything you have endured. You are special and unique. Your wonderful spirit is the beauty that the Lord has placed within you. It will outlast any other attraction you may possess. Nurture your spirit with the Word of God. It will strengthen you when you need it the most. See yourself as God sees you. You are the design who delivers human life. Without you, where would we be? You are carrying the next great Physician, Musician, Athlete, President, and World Changer – act like it. The Creator has placed you in the life of your man to help him develop and grow into all who He desires for him to be.

Do not look at your position as if it has no value because it does. Your position is more valuable than you may know. You are his engine. Your words fuel his movements. You are his ear. You listen to him as he shares his concerns and dreams. You are his counselor. You give him great advice. You are his eyes. You see what he does not see. You are his parachute. Your prayers keep him safe. The Lord blesses your man as you cover him in prayer.

Many of my blessings have been filtered through my wife to me. She has given me godly advice that has pointed me in the right direction. The Lord continues to use her to teach me, "What Does A Real MAN Look Like?" He will utilize you to do the same for you man. Keep your head up. You are the vessel who the Lord loves. You were created from a place of protection. I want to encourage you to protect your man daily by praying for him and showing him the love of God. Your encouragement helps him with his daily transformation.

Here is a prayer for you: Father, thank You for showing "Raymond" and I how to protect each other. I thank You for teaching us that we are equal. Thank You for opening our eyes and allowing us to see this relationship as You see it. "Raymond" is my protector and I am his supporter. We are a team. I will do all I can to shield "Raymond," and I am thankful that "Raymond" is doing all he can to shield me. Thanks for making me the "Suitable Helper." Strengthen me in this special role. I am grateful that "Raymond" appreciates and respects my role in our relationship. Thanks for giving us security in You, in Jesus' name. Amen.

Reflection

Please take the time to journal your questions and comments as a powerful way to track your progress. These moments are when you take the time to reflect on what you have learned in this chapter and express your thoughts. What did you learn from this chapter? Do you view your woman as your equal? Do you appreciate her opinion? Do you attempt to change her? How do you view your woman? Do you respect her differences? How has this chapter changed the way you view her? What are you going to do to let her know that she is your equal and that you cherish her?

Here is a confession for you to pray: I am a man of excellence, and I excel in all that I do. I think big, and I get big results because I serve a big God. I go the extra mile with joy to honor God and my woman. I am a man of high standards just like Joseph, and I will maintain my standards no matter the circumstances. I am an overcomer; therefore, I succeed in all that I do. Thank You, Father, for helping me with this transformation. I am a real man, and I will demonstrate this stance daily, in Jesus' name. Amen.

See if you remember what you read in this chapter.

The woman was created from what part of the body?

_____ _____ _____.

What does this part of the body represent?

_____ _____ _____ _____ _____ _____ _____ _____ _____ _____.

A Real Man Is Considerate

Matthew 1:25 **But he had no union with her as her husband until she had borne her firstborn Son;** and he called His name Jesus {Amplified Bible}.

A real man is considerate. A real man does not consider himself if he is the only one who benefits from the thought. Men tend to put lots of focus on sex. Most of us take great pleasure in being sexually intimate with our woman. There are several different types and levels of intimacy, but we usually prefer sexual affection over the others. Imagine not being able to have sex with your woman for nearly one year {nine months of pregnancy plus six to eight weeks of recovery}. Joseph faced this challenge, and he thought not of himself. How difficult would it be if you were faced with this issue? How would you handle this test? Where would your focus be? How would you make your woman feel? Would you demonstrate sensitivity or is your bond ruled by sex? Would this situation be an invitation for an affair? Would your woman feel frustration or compassion from you?

Joseph was tested in every area of his life, especially in the relationship he had with Mary, and he passed the test with flying colors. You will also be tested in every area of your life including the relationship you have with your woman. Will you pass or fail the test? Everything of value will be tried or put through the fire at some point. Please understand that the trials are not here to destroy you but to purify you. The Lord uses difficulties to bring out the very best in us. All of the circumstances that I have faced produced who I am today. The difficult challenges made me better, stronger, patient, and considerate. Without these events, I would have remained in the same old place. It is safe to say that obstacles transport us from an awful place to a better place. One of the greatest challenges that I ever encountered was the death of my mother. She was quite young when she died, and I was so hurt. During this hardship, I thought that tomorrow would never come. The discomfort left me at a stand-still for what seemed to be an eternity so I sought the Lord like never before, and He found me. People usually say, "I found the Lord." Is the Lord lost or are we lost without Him? We do not find the Lord. The Lord finds us. The Lord is our Shepherd, and He is always calling for His sheep. "My sheep listen to my voice; I know them, and they follow me" {John 10:27NLT}.   As you are faced with troubling issues, the first Person you call on is God. How many times has something bad happened to you and your first thoughts were, "Oh, My God?"

"Oh, my God" is what Joseph said when he was confronted with Mary's unexpected pregnancy, and the Lord answered his cry and made everything clear. He is the answer to all of our calls. Without Him, the troubling matters control our lives. Difficult situations are your friend not your enemy. How you view challenges is a key principle to true success. If you perceive life's tests as negative experiences, then negativity is what you are going to receive. If you perceive life's tests as a positive opportunity, then it will purify you and make you stronger. When you were in school, you were given exams to prepare you for the next grade level. The exams proved to you and your teacher that you were ready for graduation. Issues are exams that prepare you for the next level of living and graduation. You cannot graduate without passing a test.

Like Joseph and Mary, my wife and I met a similar situation when she was pregnant. We went to the doctor for a routine visit, and he discovered some complications in the pregnancy. His first words were, "You two can no longer have sex if you want to have this child. If you choose to continue to have sex, there is a great chance you will lose the baby." Since my wife was only six weeks pregnant, this announcement was really difficult for me. As most

176

men do, I really enjoy having sex. What do you do when something you crave for so much is right before you, but you are not allowed to satisfy the craving? Similar to Adam and Eve, many of us feed our desires and consider the consequences after the fact. This lesson was my advanced crash course on consideration. I was not ready for this challenging adjustment, but I was forced into readiness. For forty weeks we abstained, and as a result, I discovered bonding to a different degree. I learned how to connect to Katrina's mind and spirit. I realized the value of her conversation, smile, and presence. A simple touch of her hands meant so much more to me, a hug was a big deal, and her smile pierced my soul. I understood her on another level and in different ways. This experience defined closeness for me. Genuine love covers all aspects of a relationship.

Notice what my initial concerns were after the doctor delivered the news to us. I considered not my wife or our baby. I thought of myself only. The Creator utilized this occasion to redirect my focus, and He aimed it towards my wife and unborn child. Her pregnancy taught me how to love her based on God's standards and eliminated the selfish ways I once had. This opportunity purified me and made me a better person. It shifted my attention to the other areas that I was neglecting. Therefore, I transformed from a selfish man to a considerate man. The complications in the pregnancy were a hidden blessing in disguised. Thank You, Jesus!

The Father rewards those who are able to overcome challenging circumstances. When Moses overcame his fears, he was rewarded and eventually delivered the Jews out of bondage {Exodus 5}. When David overcame Goliath, he was rewarded and eventually became the king {1st Samuel 17}. When Jesus overcame His struggles in the Garden of Gethsemane, we were all rewarded with eternal life contingent upon our belief {Matthew 26}. Do you see the pattern here? All three men overcame their battles because they did not consider themselves for the sake of others. Once you are a considerate man, you will help your woman to overcome the difficulties of life, and the Creator will reward you. The Lord blessed Katrina and me because we conquered our selfishness, and He awarded us with our beautiful daughter, Skyy. I cannot tell you how she has changed our lives. We call her "The Glue" as she holds our family closer together. Her existence shows what the power of consideration is all about – love. Skyy is God's promise to my wife and me. Due to our obedience, we are able to taste the fruit of our actions. "If you are willing and obedient, you shall eat the good of the land" {Isaiah 1:19NKJV}. Let me encourage you to stay on the course and finish the race that you have started with your woman. A real man is considerate and is not concerned with how he starts the race, but rather, he is concerned with how he finishes the marathon. This is what a real man looks like and does.

Ladies, you were created by God to be considerate. For this reason, you have the ability to carry and have children. The Creator formed females with a motherly and nurturing spirit. You do not consider yourself while you are pregnant. You are not worried about the symptoms or the changes to your body. Your focus is directed towards the baby's needs and comfort. Your thoughtfulness is quite a gift. You have a human growing inside of you, shifting your organs around, changing your appearance, and yet, your heart is centered on the pregnancy. Amazing! There is not another creation on the planet more familiar with transformation than you. Change is always happening in and around you. Therefore, you are known as "the backbone of society." God has blessed you with the ability to demonstrate consideration in a special way. Your ability to care for others is the beauty of being a woman. You experience change when your child is growing on the inside of you. You face even more changes as your infant begins to develop outside of your womb. Motherhood is not limited to giving birth. By the Creator's special design, you are a nurturer, and you have performed motherly duties to someone at some point. I am not ashamed to admit that my wife picked up where my mother left off. She nurtured me into real manhood.

Have you noticed the changes in your man from the time you first met him? When you first met your man, his views and actions may have been different than what they are today. As time progressed with your support, he began to grow into real manhood. You were instrumental in this growth because you considered him first before yourself. Your thoughtfulness was a seed, and now the harvest is the changes that your man is displaying. Because of your sacrifices, you, your man, and children are living under the same roof. Your efforts have and are helping your man with his transformation. I salute women as a great example of the love of God. You are not selfish, but rather, you are generous for the sake of the bigger picture. You are a blessing to society and mankind.

Here is a prayer for you: Father, empower "Jackson" and I with a heart to please You first and then each other. Jesus and Joseph have shown us the power of consideration, and I am thankful for these examples. I personally will follow their lead and always consider what is best for everyone. Thank You for touching the heart of "Jackson" and inspiring him to do the same for the betterment of us and our family, in Jesus' name. Amen.

Reflection

Please take the time to journal your questions and comments as a powerful way to track your progress. These moments are when you take the time to reflect on what you have learned in this chapter and express your thoughts. What did you learn from this chapter? Are you a thoughtful person? Does your woman complain about you being inconsiderate? Is considerate a word that people utilize to describe you? What have you learned in this chapter that will help you to become more considerate? If you had a slice of your favorite cake and your woman asked you for a bite, would you offer her a bite or half of the cake?

Considerate is an adjective defined on Dictionary.com as: "Considerate: Showing kindly awareness or regard for another's feelings, circumstances, etc." Are you anywhere in this definition?

Here is a confession for you to pray: I am a man of excellence, and I excel in all that I do. I think big, and I get big results because I serve a big God. I go the extra mile with joy to honor God and my woman. I am a man of high standards just like Joseph, and I will maintain my standards no matter the circumstances. I am an overcomer; therefore, I succeed in all that I do. Thank You, Father, for helping me with this transformation. I am a real man, and I will demonstrate this stance daily, in Jesus' name. Amen.

See if you remember what you read in this chapter.

A considerate person is an overcomer. Overcomers are always

_____ _____ _____ _____ _____ _____ _____ _____.

A Real Man Loves Without Limitations

A real man loves without limitations. Just as a woman's body is available to house, carry, and deliver life, a man's body must be available to house, carry, and deliver love.

We are all born with the ability to love. Our capacity to love grows as we nurture it from within. Has your ability to love grown since birth or is it still in its infancy stages? Love is alive. Everything that has life must be feed. If love is not feed, it will surely die. What do you have on the menu of your heart? Love must be fed with more love. Nothing else would satisfy its craving. Unlike the human stomach, you will not have heartache if you stuff your heart with endless love.

Love needs a home. It is often stated, "There is no place like home." Does your heart represent the comfort of a cozy home? What does the welcome mat of your heart look like? Is it inviting or uninviting? A child develops strongly in a healthy womb, and love develops strongly in a healthy heart. Prenatal vitamins are vital during a woman's pregnancy. What pills are you taking to secure the love that God has placed within you? The Gospel is the vitamin of recommendation. Chewing on the Gospel is the way to feed your heart the proper nutrients. This meal reconstructs a person's heart. The love of God is different than the love of man. When man says, "I cannot love anymore. I have reached my capacity to love. My love tank is on empty." God says, "Love never gives up, never loses faith, is always hopeful, and endures through every circumstance."

Love accompanies you wherever you go. As a child is attached to his mother in the womb, love is attached to the man who embodies it. When love is your ruling emotion, everyone you meet is blessed by your presence. A person who is a transporter of love has the ability to be a bright light for someone who is in darkness. A person who is a transporter of love has the ability to be a spotter for someone who is struggling under heaviness. A person who is a transporter of love has the ability to be a lifeline for someone who is ready to give up and pull the plug. A woman who is visibly six months pregnant does not have to announce that she is pregnant. A man who is a carrier of love does not have to announce that he is a carrier of love. When you are a carrier of love, everyone notices it.

To be a transporter of love means that you are carrying something good {love}, and in turn, you are removing something bad from the people you touch {hate, stress, conflicts, etc.} Many of us are transporters of love, but we are not relieving ourselves of the baggage that we have removed from others. If you are carrying fifty pounds on your back, and I take it from you, the weight does not disappear. The weight was transported from you to me. Have you ever made a sad person feel better? Have you ever replaced a person's tears with a smile? This revelation is known as the law of transfer. Yes, it is good to be the carrier of love; however, it is also good to unload the burdens that you have removed by giving them to Jesus. For this reason, Jesus instructed us to, "Cast all your anxiety on him because he cares for you" {1st Peter 5:7NIV}.

Love has to be delivered at the right time. Many of us are not delivering love at the right time. If you are around people and detect they are not feeling their best that is the appropriate time to deliver a loving conversation. If you are around your friend and notice a frown on his face that is the right time to make him smile. If you are around your woman and feel like she is in need of a hug that is the suitable time to embrace her like your favorite teddy bear. The appropriate time to deliver love is now. Lots of us are putting off what we can do today for tomorrow. "Do not say to your neighbor, "Go, and come back, and tomorrow I will give it," when you have it with you" {Proverbs 3:28NKJV}. Imagine how Mary felt when Joseph approached her and delivered the news, "Mary, I have heard from God regarding our pregnancy. I accept you and the baby. I love you and the baby. Let's be a family." There is nothing like a "special delivery." Notice the word "special." Are you excited when you order something and get that special knock on your door from the mailman? Think about how exciting it is for the people who have labeled you Mr. Special Delivery. These people look forward to your presence because you are like a breath of fresh air. You are the life of the party. You help them to recognize how special they are, and they feel special whenever you are around. Ultimately, you are a representation of the Spirit who lives on the inside of you. You are the house, carrier, and deliverer of love to the world. The world needs "Love, sweet love." A real man loves without limitations.

Lots of men struggle with the concept of unconditional love. Loving to this extent is often viewed as a weakness. The influences around us have painted an inaccurate photograph into our mind. There is nothing weak about unconditional love. At first, I struggled to love to this degree. I displayed love based on how I felt, the way that I was treated, or by my particular mood. According to God, love is unconditional. Unconditional love has nothing to do with our feelings, the way we are treated, or our particular moods. We are not living a fulfilled life if we love based on those standards. Remember, we are not responsible for what other people do, but we are responsible for what we do. Love does not have limitations. Love is as solid as a rock and goes beyond all boundaries.

In the 1st Corinthians book of the Bible is a lesson often called the "Love Scripture." I have taken the love Scripture and replaced the word "Love" with "I." This practice has really changed my life and outlook, and I know it is going to do the same for you.

Here is the Scripture: "Love is patient and kind. Love is not jealous or boastful or proud or rude. It does not demand its own way. It is not irritable, and it keeps no record of being wronged. It does not rejoice about injustice but rejoices whenever the truth wins out. Love never gives up, never loses faith, is always hopeful, and endures through every circumstance" {1st Corinthians 13:4-7NLT}.

Now, here is the "I" version. Read this Scripture aloud so you can experience the power of these amazing statements. "I am patient and kind. I am not jealous or boastful or proud or rude. I do not demand my own way. I am not irritable, and I keep no record of being wronged. I do not rejoice about injustice, but I rejoice whenever the truth wins out. I never give up, I never lose faith, I am always hopeful, and I endure through every circumstance." What you just read is the Creator's love towards us. It is His desire for us to love to this degree. Change does not occur by itself. Your involvement and application is required.

Here are the descriptions of three different kinds of love. Agape is unconditional love. It is selfless love of one person for another without sexual implications. It is love that is spiritual in nature {Ref: wordnetweb.princeton.edu/perl/webwn}. Eros is also called marital love, passionate love with sensual desire and longing {Ref: en.wikipedia.org/wiki/Eros_love}. Philia is for friendships or affectionate love {Ref: http://en.wikipedia.org/wiki/Greek words for love}. It is God's desire that we strive for agape love because agape love displays the unconditional love of God.

We spend countless hours on a treadmill and in the weight room striving to perfect our physical health and appearance, but we lose our patience the first time something happens that we do not like. Does this behavior display agape love? What is the first description of love according to 1st Corinthians 13? How are you able to push to exercise for thirty additional minutes even though you are fatigued, but you quit two seconds following a disappointment? How can you go the extra mile on the treadmill and not even complete a mile when it comes to demonstrating agape love? Why do we value our body more than our spirit? If you do not learn to love without limitations, you are going to lose your woman in more ways than one. She needs to be freely loved. She dreams of this desire daily. She will not be satisfied with anything short of one hundred percent of your love. My wife is a different person because of the agape love which I display to her. As a result, we both are happier.

In the past, I thought I was a loving person in spite of my faults. My definition of love was far from God's definition. It was my remixed version which needed mastering. At this point, you have no excuses. Agape love does not make excuses. Now, you know how to express real love. I pray you begin to apply these principles immediately so that the healing and restoration process can begin. A real man welcomes the agape type of love. He knows that any other choice is not love at all. A real man loves without limitations.

Ladies, I strongly recommend that you make it a good habit to read the tailored love Scripture aloud as much as possible. Recite it with your man early in the morning and at night before you both go to bed. My wife and I have applied this principle to our marriage, and it keeps us in alignment with the Lord and each other. We base our union on the Word of God, and we hold each other accountable to His word. The moment you replace the word "love" with the word "I," it holds you accountable because you have made it your own. I promise you that if you make this concept a part of your life, you are going to lose any negative weight that you might be carrying and become healthier in every aspect of your life. Remember, it is all about freedom. Agape love is a great way to obtain and declare your liberation. The experience will be liberating for you both.

One of the best ways to show Agape love to your man is by reminding him of his past victories. Lots of men are under pressure because of our drive to succeed. As you well know, success does not come without work, dedication, and failures. Normally, we do not have a problem with the work or dedication. It is the failures that discourage us. That is why it is very important for you to remind your man of his accomplishments. My wife reminds me of my accomplishments to this very day, and it is fuel to my engine. This loving act is just what God does. He does not remind us about the times that we have failed. Quite the opposite, He reminds us about the times that we have succeeded. I encourage you to implement this approach daily.

The story of David and Abigail as found in the Bible is fascinating. David was at a low point in his life, on the run, and living in the wilderness. David had a conversation with Abigail which changed the course of his life. Before they had this life changing talk, he was very upset, and he had promised to kill everyone in her household. This conversation was absolutely amazing. Abigail was able to put out the raging inferno within David by reminding him of his victory over the giant Goliath. "Though man is risen up to pursue you and to seek your life, yet the life of my lord shall be bound in the living bundle with the Lord your God. And the lives of your enemies—them shall He sling out as out of the center of a sling" {1st Samuel 25AMP}. The word "sling" in the Scripture is referring to the time that David defeated the giant Goliath {Read 1st Samuel Chapter 17}. This loving conversation impressed David so much that he married Abigail when the time permitted. Abigail went from being a normal woman to being the queen because she knew how to talk to her man.

Ladies, when you show Agape love to your man by reminding him of his victories, it benefits you as well. What sort of impression do you believe this conversation will have on your man? "Honey, you cannot lose. There is a champion on the inside of you. Do you remember when you were promoted at your job? Do you remember when you helped me during a testing period of my life? Do you remember when we did not have the proper tools, but you still found a way to hang up those curtains in the living room? Do you remember when you broke those tackles and scored the touchdown to help your team win the game? The person who succeeded then is the person who will succeed now! I love and believe in you." This powerful victory talk will remove any sense of failure that your man may be feeling.

Jesus is our earthly example of Agape love. Before Jesus started His ministry, He went before His cousin, John the Baptist, and was baptized. Baptism symbolizes death to the natural man so that the spiritual man can take the leading role {Read Matthew Chapter 3}. In order for a person to exhibit agape love, he must learn how to love from beneath the surface. Many of us fall in love with what we see and never truly fall in love with what we do not see – a person's heart. "So we fix our eyes not on what is seen, but on what is unseen, since what is seen is temporary, but what is unseen is eternal" {2nd Corinthians 4:18NIV}.

Agape love is in operation when a person is humble. Jesus humbled Himself when He allowed John to baptize Him. In reality, John did not want to do it. "Then Jesus came from Galilee to the Jordan to be baptized by John. But John tried to deter him, saying, "I need to be baptized by you, and do you come to me?" Jesus replied, "Let it be so now; it is proper for us to do this to fulfill all righteousness." Then John consented" {Matthew 3:13-15NIV}. Finally, Jesus did not begin His ministry until He was filled with the Spirit of God. Invite the Holy Spirit into your heart and nurture that relationship daily by meditating on the Word of God. Dying to your instinctive habits, loving from beneath the surface, humility, and the Holy Spirit form the combined principles which display agape love.

What your man says or does should not stop you from displaying agape love. The agape love that my wife displayed to me changed my life. If the love of God changed me, it will certainly change anyone. God did not command us to like each other, but He did command us to love each other.

Agape love extends your life. It protects your immune and nervous system. It is beneficial for your overall health. Your life lengthens due to a higher level of patience. Patience works for you and not against you since you are able to go the extra mile. Going the extra mile makes you healthier. Agape love gives you balance because your physical and spiritual health are one in full operation.

Here is a prayer for you: Father, "Jesse" and I are patient and kind. "Jesse" and I are not jealous or boastful or proud or rude. "Jesse" and I do not demand our own way. "Jesse" and I are not irritable, and "Jesse" and I keep no record of being wronged. "Jesse" and I do not rejoice about injustice, but "Jesse" and I rejoice whenever the truth wins out. "Jesse" and I never give up, never lose faith, and are always hopeful. "Jesse" and I endure through every circumstance, in Jesus' name. Amen.

Reflection

Please take the time to journal your questions and comments as a powerful way to track your progress. These moments are when you take the time to reflect on what you have learned in this chapter and express your thoughts. What did you learn from this chapter? Can you honestly say that you understood love prior to this chapter? What are you going to do from this day to display the Agape type of love? What challenges do you have regarding living a sacrificed life? Do you view this range of love as a weakness? Does loving to this degree make you feel vulnerable? Have you ever said, "I am not going to give her all of my heart?" Have you ever stated, "I am not going to fall deeply in love with her?" Have you ever announced, "I care about you but only to a certain limit?" If you answered "yes" to the last three questions, were you truly displaying love?

Here is a confession for you to pray: I am a man of excellence and I excel in all that I do. I think big, and I get big results because I serve a big God. I go the extra mile with joy to honor God and my woman. I am a man of high standards just like Joseph, and I will maintain my standards no matter the circumstances. I am an overcomer; therefore, I succeed in all that I do. Thank You, Father, for helping me with this transformation. I am a real man, and I will demonstrate this stance daily, in Jesus' name. Amen.

See if you remember what you read in this chapter.

How many sorts of love did I describe in this chapter?

_____.

Where Was The Beef?

There are many events in the story of Joseph and Mary that stand out to me. One important point is that there is no mention of an argument. I find the absent of a dispute to be very interesting as I do not know too many men who would have responded the way Joseph did. We can learn from what was said in the Bible, and we can learn even more from what was not said. When the problem is too big, take your concerns to God following Joseph's example. Joseph did not argue, scream, or become violent, but rather, he remained silent and took his concerns to the Lord. Joseph would not have believed Mary if she had told him she was pregnant but remained a virgin. If Mary had told him that, her statement would have added fuel to the fire. More than likely, he would have believed Mary was lying to him and insulting his intelligence. Would you believe your woman if she told you she was impregnated by the Holy Spirit? Would you feel she was lying and insulting your intelligence? It is acceptable to be angry as long as you do not allow the anger to control you. "Be angry, and do not sin" do not let the sun go down on your wrath, nor give place to the devil" {Ephesians 4-26:27NKJV}.

Take your concerns to God. At times, I am unsure about a matter or my wife cannot explain how and why a situation occurred. Instead of arguing or trying to squeeze the truth out of her, I present my uncertainties to the Creator. People love to be believed and hate to be doubted. In the past, I may have pressed her for the truth. My smothering made her feel as though I did not trust her. My decision to prosecute her was not a wise choice. It added to the frustration. Did my actions represent love? I now believe in remaining calm and having a comfortable environment. When peace is absent, chaos rules, and I absolutely hate disorder.

Why do you need to present your issues to the Creator? As God did with Joseph, He will comfort and empower you. Again, we know Joseph had some level of peace because he was able to sleep. Are you able to sleep once problems have consumed you or are you up tossing and turning all night? In the Lord's presence, we find all of the answers to our questions. I believe Joseph slept because he trusted the Lord and sought His guidance. This is what a real man looks like and does. Why do you need to take your concerns to the Lord? He represents truth. When you give your affairs to Him, He blesses you with His truth. Anxieties can imprison you; however, the truth breaks the chains and makes you free. When you are seeking the integrity of a matter and it appears like your woman has wronged you, take your doubts to the Creator. Remember, the way circumstances appear to be and how they really are can be two different realities.

Why should you give your problems to God? Scripture tells us, "He is the Spirit of truth" and "He will guide you into all the truth." "But when He, the Spirit of Truth {the Truth-giving Spirit} comes, He will guide you into all the Truth {the whole, full Truth}. For He will not speak His own message {on His own authority}; but He will tell whatever He hears {from the Father; He will give the message that has been given to Him}, and He will announce and declare to you the things that are to come {that will happen in the future}" {John 16:13AMP}. Here is an example of surrendering a problem to the Holy Spirit in your daily life. There are times when I misplace my keys. At that point, I sit down and say, "Holy Spirit, what is the truth about the keys that I cannot find?" At that moment, I move onto something else knowing the location will be revealed to me, and it works every time. He gives me a mental vision of the keys and their whereabouts. He is concerned about everything regarding you. Once you follow His light, He will never leave you in the dark.

Where was the beef? Since the Lord dwelled in their hearts, I believe there was no argument. Joseph was a godly man, and Mary was a godly woman. For this reason, the beef was not a factor. If it was a factor, it would have been mentioned in the Bible. The Creator is calmness in the middle of turmoil. Disputes are handled differently once He is the ruling force in our lives. He removes burdens. He removed the issues that Joseph and Mary faced by revealing the truth. He will certainly remove the issues from your relationship. Because of the alignment of Joseph's will with God's will, the Creator spoke, and Joseph listened. This willingness is needed from you as well to experience growth in your relationship. Does your relationship seem hopeless? Do you believe it is dead? Grant the Lord admission and see what happens. I thought my marriage was over, but when I let Him in, He turned everything around.

Where was the beef? Harmful reactions make matters worse. The Lord utilized this story to illustrate this truth. Remaining calm always works out for our good. Negative responses are terrible for the heart possibly leading to a heart attack or stroke. Have you ever felt so angry that your heart seemed to be coming out of your chest? The wise choice is to maintain your composure.

As you remain calm, you can hear from your heart {God}. The heart is God's podium. He speaks from there and declares the truth to your spirit. Why should you listen to your heart? It warns you when negative emotions are attempting to control you. The warnings signs include a rapid heartbeat, shortness of breath, sweating, blurry vision, etc. These symptoms are signs that a "Time-Out" is needed. You need to pay close attention to your heart rate. You maintain a healthy heart rate by including the Lord in the beef. Often, when we are faced with challenges, we exclude God from the happenings; however, we gladly invite Him into the events after everything blows up. If we consult with the Creator during the challenging moments, the consequences of our poor decisions would be avoided.

Our nervous system is negatively impacted when our emotions are out of control. A deer gazing at a headlight and an emotional person share this truth in common, they are not able to function at some point. Have you ever watched a scary movie and said, "Why can't she open the door. What's stopping him from driving the car?" The answer is cortisol. When a person is upset, their capacity to think clearly is compromised. Their brain releases the chemical cortisol. Cortisol is a chemical that increases stress and frustration. The results are the unbalance that many of us witness on the movie screen. Once released, it remains with a person for about twenty minutes presenting a serious attack on the immune and nervous system. All destructive emotions can have this impact on you.

We need to guard our heart. "Guard your heart above all else, for it determines the course of your life" {Proverbs 4:23NLT}. Our heart is valuable. It can be stolen. We protect it by keeping the beef on the grill where it belongs. Beef has no place in relationships. The minute we allow the beef into our lives, it grills our organs and dries us. When we are emotional, our body temperature rises resulting in a loss of water. Since water makes up about seventy-five percent of the human brain, we all need water to function effectively. We were not created to be cooked or dehydrated. Our heart was not designed to carry beef. The human heart was constructed to pump blood throughout the body. It is the storage place of our God given treasure {love}. If negative emotions rule, the heart stands a greater chance of being damage. You know you are listening to your heart:

1.   when you remove yourself from people who may be causing you stress;

2.   when your mouth does not feel dry;

3.   once you can hear and see clearly;

4.   when your breathing remains at a normal rate;

5.   as you apply the principles you have learned throughout this book.

Now do you see the importance of granting God access to your life and relationship? Once He is directing your steps, you gain from it in more ways than you can imagine. Our heart leads us in the right direction when we listen to its navigation. We are lost when the voice of our heart is muted. The frustration adds undesirable weight. Pressure can burst pipes while volcanoes erupt from the build-up of tension. What form of damage do you think stress causes to the heart? Pay attention to the signs. A heart attack means the signals were ignored. To maintain a healthy heart, master your emotions and keep the beef on the grill where it belongs.

A healthy heart secures a productive life. For an adult, a normal resting heart rate ranges from 60 to 100 beats a minute. For a well-trained athlete, an average resting heart rate may be closer to 40 beats a minute. For healthy adults, a lower resting heart rate generally implies more efficient heart function and better cardiovascular fitness. Ideally, you want your heart rate to be between 60 to 90 beats per minute. The normal resting heart rate for men is 70 beats per minute and 75 beats per minute for women. How you handle your emotions determines your heart rate.

Ladies, there are many lessons to learn from Mary. She did not argue with Joseph, try to prove her innocence, or defend her character. How was she empowered by not speaking? How difficult is it for you not to speak and defend yourself? Mary was a woman of great wisdom. She knew her words would have made matters worse; therefore, she remained silent and relied on God to speak for her as He did. Her approach is so amazing. What she did not say was more impactful than anything she could have said. When you find yourself in a place where you do not know what to say, say nothing at all, and the Communicator will communicate for you. Mary was strong, confident, and courageous in her silence. While Mary said nothing, God was speaking to her heart. His heartfelt conversation is what helped her, and it will surely help you. Are you listening to your heart? The Lord is your Defense Attorney, and He has never lost a trial. "My dear children, I am writing this to you so that you will not sin. But if anyone does sin, we have an advocate who pleads our case before the Father. He is Jesus Christ, the one who is truly righteous. He himself is the sacrifice that atones for our sins—and not only our sins but the sins of all the world" {1st John 2:1-2NLT}.

Since women are great communicators, I know remaining silent may be difficult. Make the decision to learn when to speak and when not to speak. By doing so, you will be displaying the control and discipline Mary displayed. Implementing this decision keeps the beef out of your home. Every action does not require a response nor is worthy of one. If your man is not acting right, pleasantly ignore him. Let him be at that party all by himself. Let God take care of the drama. My wife still applies this principle today, and it always works. For instance, if I am frustrated regarding an issue, she speaks to me about it once. After she discusses the concern with me, she remains silent and so do I. We have come to the point of allowing God to fix our differences. The truth is life is too precious. Therefore, I would rather spend my time grilling beef instead of having it in my marriage. I do not want the negativity around me or in me. For this reason, I constantly feed myself the Word of God. If you constantly feed yourself the Word of God, nothing but His words would come out of your mouth.

Every relationship has a fuse in it, and the fuse has no power until it is lit. Do not light the fuse by entertaining the beef. The next time your man attempts to draw you into an argument, go into your refrigerator, grab a piece of beef, and tell him, "This beef is the only beef that I am entertaining. Now, how do you want your dinner cooked, honey?" Can you imagine the impact this action will have on him? Humility and love opens the door of your man's heart. Once it is open, God takes care of the rest. I would much rather live in peace than war. I believe you will agree with me.

Here is a prayer for you: Father, thank You for teaching "Antonio" and me when to speak and when not to speak. I am grateful that there is no beef in our relationship You cannot remove. I pray for Your constant guidance. Teach us how to rest as Joseph did. Show us how to remain silent as Mary did. Thank You for speaking to us and for us. Thank You for the Holy Spirit. He is our guide to all truth. Thanks for teaching us how to listen to our hearts and master our reactions. Thanks for providing us with the right words at the right time. Your words are forever true. "Antonio" and me we will feast on them continuously, in Jesus' name. Amen.

Reflection

Please take the time to journal your questions and comments as a powerful way to track your progress. These moments are when you take the time to reflect on what you have learned in this chapter and express your thoughts. What did you learn from this chapter? How important is it for you to win an argument? Do you struggle when it comes to giving your concerns to God? Do you believe the Lord will reveal the truth to you regarding your doubts? How do you know if it is time for a "Time-Out?" What is the ideal heart rate for you? What should you do if you begin to sweat, have blurred vision, or have distorted hearing? Why is it important for to remain hydrated? How does dehydration impact your brain? What chemical is released into your body when you are emotional? How long does the chemical remain with you once it is released?

Here is a confession for you to pray: I am a man of excellence, and I excel in all that I do. I think big, and I get big results because I serve a big God. I go the extra mile with joy to honor God and my woman. I am a man of high standards just like Joseph, and I will maintain my standards no matter the circumstances. I am an overcomer; therefore, I succeed in all that I do. Thank You, Father, for helping me with this transformation. I am a real man, and I will demonstrate this stance daily, in Jesus' name. Amen.

See if you remember what you read in this chapter.

What two systems are attacked when Cortisol is released?

____ ____ ____ ____ ____ ____ & ____ ____ ____ ____
____ ____ ____.

What Determined Joseph and Mary's Success?

God is absolutely amazing! He placed "The Secrets" to a successful relationship in the story of Joseph and Mary. Why did God put these secrets in this story? God is saying all relationships can succeed when He is included in them. God knows there are no perfect relationships or people. Therefore, God utilized this remarkable story with all of its complicated issues to teach us all how to win the battles in our relationships.

Before Joseph and Mary united in marriage, they were initially united to God. Before they were physically intimate with each other, they were spiritually intimate with God. Here is "The" key principle to this amazing story and "THE" main ingredient for a successful relationship. A real man must be committed to God "in the beginning" in order for the relationship to work between himself and his woman. Committing to a person is a good thing; however, there is nothing like committing to the Creator. In reality, I do not believe people can seriously commit to anyone or anything unless they are first able to seriously commit to God.

In this story, the Lord shows us the magnitude of dedication required for any union to succeed. Think about everything Joseph and Mary endured. Reflect on the truth that Joseph was not intimate with Mary until after Jesus was born, and yet, their relationship is our model. The Creator expects for us to learn from them and apply what we have learned. If men followed the standards set by Joseph, society would change for the better. This trial taught Joseph how to love Mary from the inside out. He loved her mind, spirit, and conversation before he was allowed to love her physically. He understood how to appreciate her on a completely different level. Many of us are not fulfilling the commitments in our relationships to this degree. Sacrifice is an unavoidable road. You will not experience God's will without crossing this path. "Then He said to them all, "If anyone desires to come after Me, let him deny himself, and take up his cross daily, and follow Me. For whoever desires to save his life will lose it, but whoever loses his life for My sake will save it. For what profit is it to a man if he gains the whole world, and is himself destroyed or lost?" {Luke 9:23-25NKJV}.

Men, many of us love our woman's physical features putting little or no focus on her mental and spiritual qualities. There is nothing wrong with loving your woman's physical features; however, they should not outweigh her mind and spirit. Her beauty is going to flee one day, but her mind and spirit will become more attractive with time. "Charm and grace are deceptive, and beauty is vain {because it is not lasting}, but a woman who reverently and worshipfully fears the Lord, she shall be praised!" {Proverbs 31:30AMP}.

Quite a few men are trading one beautiful woman for another beautiful woman. No wonder couples are breaking up constantly, and the divorce rate is skyrocketing. Society's mentality is the man with the prettiest woman has the best trophy. Women are not trophies but are the Father's gift to mankind. God shows us in the Bible the building blocks that are required to establish a healthy view of women. Unfortunately, many of us continue to neglect His instructions.

What determined the success of Joseph and Mary's relationship? The commitment they both had for the Lord was their building block. Faithfulness to this degree represents a strong foundation, self-control, and honorable character. First, everything we believe is built on either a strong or weak foundation. How do you know if your foundation is strong or weak? Whatever you establish based on the Scriptures is a solid foundation, and whatever you establish independent from the

Scriptures is unreliable. "Unless the Lord builds a house, the work of the builders is wasted {Psalm 127:1NLT}. Anything you construct independent from God will crumble and fall. Everything that I established in the past without God failed including the initial relationship with my wife. However, when we both completely surrendered to the Creator, everything began to turn around.

Why is it important to commit your relationship to the Father first and build it with His guidance? Committing your relationship to the Lord gives you the boundaries and the guidelines to true success in your union. For example, if you are driving sixty miles per hour in a twenty-five mile per hour zone, you are breaking the law and will be punished if you are caught. The speed limit sign on the road is your boundary and guide pertaining to the speed of your car. Joseph cruised and did not speed. His commitment to the Lord was the sign he followed. He stayed on course and did not break God's law. The Creator has to be the driver and the driving force in your relationship in order for it to succeed. He knows when to slow down and speed up, He will never break any law, and He is dedicated to your safety and success. Dedication to this degree leaves the negative emotions on the curb of the street, and at that point, the truth becomes your chauffeur. I no longer have emotional setbacks. As a result, my wife and I are set on cruise control. Thank God! What changed is the level of our dedication to God. The Author of our faith is always our number one priority. We do not do anything independently from the Father. We pray about everything. This commitment was demonstrated by Joseph and Mary. Since the Lord cannot fail, you cannot fail once you fully commit to Him. A real man knows he has to obligate all of himself to the Lord: emotionally, financially, mentally, physically, and spiritually before he can entirely devote himself to his woman. This is what a real man looks like and does.

Think about the times when you convinced yourself that it was ok to speed due to the open road or because other cars were speeding. Reflect on the moments when you were full, but you went for one more bite. Consider the instances when you persuaded yourself that your actions were acceptable, even though you knew they were not. Self-control is what Joseph displayed throughout this wonderful story. It is one of the main reasons why Joseph and Mary were successful. There is nothing like living a well-balanced, disciplined life. Discipline is the missing ingredient in the lives of so many people today leading to countless failed marriages. What do you believe most men would have done if they had been in Joseph's position? Yell, become violent, utilize curse words, and display uncontrollable anger. Why was Joseph different? What kept him focused? Self-control! Again, it is all about boundaries and guidelines. I shared with you the failures I experienced in my relationship due to my lack of self-control, and I also shared the successes I gained due to self-control. I am proud to say I am experiencing life differently every day because of my willingness to embrace self-control. I tell myself daily, "Today, you are going to display amazing self-control in all that you say and do." It feels great to know that my wife trust, believes, and cherishes me. She appreciates the poise I display day-to-day. A real man is strong because of the self-control he displays.

Relationships are lots of work, and the real you will be tested at some point. You must display honorable character in order to pass the test. Earlier in my marriage, I failed miserably by showing little patience and respect for my wife. I did not know this then, but I know this now. My impatience and disrespect not only offended my wife, but my actions also offended God. Strangely, I thought I was very polite to the Lord despite my actions. In my mind, my relationship with God was separate from my relationship with others. This belief is far from the truth. When you are faithful to the Creator and He is your foundation and guide, you will reflect that positive attitude towards others. Your character becomes razor sharp as you aim the respect that you have for God towards others. The Lord has something to say about becoming the new you, "This means that anyone who belongs to Christ has become a new person. The old life is gone; a new life has begun" {2nd Corinthians 5:17NLT}.

These are principles that I live by, and they work. My position does not mean people always respond positively towards me. Regardless of their response, I hold onto my standards. I am loyal to God, not to a person's behavior. This focus steers me in the right direction and helps me to succeed.

The Lord is entrusting us with someone of great significance. Therefore, it is the Lord's desire for us to thrive in our relationships. If we are not committed to Him from the very beginning, we are going to mishandle this special person's heart. He entrusted Joseph and Mary with Jesus. However, if they were not committed to God, they would have mishandled His "GIFT" to humanity. What priceless gift does your relationship have?

How do we know your relationship has a gift that can change the world? God blessed Joseph and Mary with "The Gift" who changed the world; therefore, God has blessed your union with a gift that can change the world as well. "For God so greatly loved and dearly prized the world that He {even} gave up His only begotten {unique} Son, so that whoever believes in {trusts in, clings to, relies on} Him shall not perish {come to destruction, be lost} but have eternal {everlasting} life" {John 3:16AMP}.

Your commitment to God does not go unnoticed. What did Joseph and Mary learn from their faithfulness? They learned how to trust God, worship God, appreciate God, rely on God, cooperate with God, and communicate with God. Look at everything they acquired because of their dedication. Do you feel you and your woman will flourish if all of these qualities are in place? Take the same steps Joseph and Mary took, and you both will surpass your wildest dreams.

Ladies, how would you rate the level of your man's commitment? Is your relationship in need of an upgrade? If it is, take your attention off of your man, and elevate your level of commitment for God. Once you do this, he will see the example of what you need from him. There is nothing better than giving a person a physical example and a mental picture. This combination changes attitudes due to the light it displays. The images you give your man are similar to a mirror. They are a constant reminder of how he should grow to develop a strong relationship with you. You can tell a person anything, but the real test is producing by your actions.

Your commitment to God removes any and all excuses. If you can commit to God and your man completely, he can be devoted at this level as well. The Bible is God's example for us all. If we are not reading, studying, and applying the Bible's teachings, our life will be in turmoil. The Lord set standards for us to follow. He would not be a loving and caring Father if He did not. "If you abide in Me, and My words abide in you, you will ask what you desire, and it shall be done for you" {John 15:7NJKV}.

It is all a matter of choices. What you are going to choose today? The Bible is your "How to Guide." The Bible is the book of never failing principles. You must first be faithful to God before you can truly receive the dedication you desire from your man. You will eventually receive what you plant. The Creator says it as such, "Don't be misled—you cannot mock the justice of God. You will always harvest what you plant" {Galatians 6:7NLT}.

If your man is not living up to his commitments, step up the level of commitment that you have for the Lord. By doing so, you will be stepping up the level of commitment that you have for your man. The Lord takes great pleasure in honor. He expects for you to honor your man even if he is not honoring you. You are a farmer, investing into his heart, and eventually, your seed will bring you exactly what you planted. Sacrifice is needed in order to obtain what you are looking for in your man. I firmly believe in this principle. If you plant a seed of commitment, you will eventually collect a harvest of commitment. However, you must do the planting in order to gather the crops. My wife did it for me. This book is part of the produce that came from her sowing.

A farmer does not plant his seeds today and look for a harvest tomorrow. Quite the opposite, a farmer plants his seeds and waits. Waiting is like a drought for many of us. The lack of commitment {water} is damaging our crops. We want it fast, and we want it now. It takes some time for people to experience a true transformation. Time is also needed to uproot the bad seeds which were planted. Time is not your enemy, but instead it is your friend. It will ripen your committed man. Your determination {soil}, God's words {seed}, endurance {sunlight}, commitment {water}, and faithfulness {patience} is needed.

Here is a prayer for you: Father, I am devoted to You and all that You require for me to do. Grant me the patience needed to fulfill Your will for my life. Help me to obtain a strong mind and attitude towards Your desires for me. I am thankful that "Terrence" is dedicated to You and to me. I am grateful that every day "Terrence" is embracing the commitment that he needs to have for our family. We are both loyal to the bond we have with You first and then with each other. Thank You for the Holy Spirit, who is the mediator in our household and the guide to all truth, in Jesus' name. Amen.

Reflection

Please take the time to journal your questions and comments as a powerful way to track your progress. These moments are when you take the time to reflect on what you have learned in this chapter and express your thoughts. What did you learn from this chapter? What must you do to live a committed godly life? Is there a particular place where you lack self-control? If so, what is that area? What do you need to do to become stronger in that area? How committed are you to your woman and children? Do you make time to bond with your woman and children? Are you more committed to work and hanging out with your friends? How much time do you spend with God? Is He your top priority?

This level of commitment is all about the location of your heart. The Lord is very much concerned with the positioning of your heart. Like Joseph, keep your heart clean, and you will begin to experience amazing success.

Here is a confession for you to pray: I am a man of excellence, and I excel in all that I do. I think big, and I get big results because I serve a big God. I go the extra mile with joy to honor God and my woman. I am a man of high standards just like Joseph, and I will maintain my standards no matter the circumstances. I am an overcomer; therefore, I succeed in all that I do. Thank You, Father, for helping me with this transformation. I am a real man, and I will demonstrate this stance daily, in Jesus' name. Amen.

See if you remember what you read in this chapter. You must have a high level of what in order to enjoy the success that Joseph and Mary obtained? _____ _____ _____ _____ _____ _____ _____ _____ _____ _____.

A Real Man Knows His Woman Well

A real man knows his woman well. Take the guessing game out of the equation by investing more time in your relationship. You are going to see the true value in your union when you thoroughly know your woman. Once I began to understand my wife deeply, disputes minimized. Honestly, my attentiveness helped us to grow closer together. What woman would not appreciate her man taking the time to learn her? Consideration is like an airplane which takes you to the deepest parts of your woman's heart. Thoughtfulness is the difference between "the dog house" and a peaceful home. Studying your woman's habits is a good decision that leads to a pleasant environment. You must recognize what makes her who she is.

In a matter of seconds, you should be able to describe her favorite color, desired restaurant, preferred food, beloved song, much loved movie, most wanted perfume, ideal designer, her passions, shoe size, and what makes her laugh, what makes her cry, what agitates her, and what is most important to her. Knowing your woman well is extremely important.

When does her menstrual cycle begin? I know you are probably saying, "Why is he asking me this?" High levels of estrogen {the female hormone} start to elevate in the first half of her menstrual cycle. As a result, this elevation causes an imbalance in her body. What does this information have to do with you? Everything! High levels of estrogen can lead to anxiety and depression and can even cause anxiety attacks. Estrogen interacts directly with the body's systems, and it creates stress responses. High estrogen levels cause hormonal fluctuations to be greater and can worsen post menstrual symptom {PMS}. Ref: http://www.ehow.com/about_5431853_symptoms-resulting-high-estrogen-levels.html

207

Now do you see the importance of knowing when her menstrual cycle begins? You may have been calling her moody because you were not aware of this information. You probably made matters worse as you began to act moody out of disgust. Knowing your woman is one thing but to know her well positions your relationship on a whole different level. Now that you have this knowledge, you can apologize to her for any harm you may have caused, become more sensitive, and exercise more love and understanding during these times. Show her how much you care by educating her with this information. Doing so will add happiness to her life since you took the time to learn more about her. Sharing what you have learned will insert balance to the imbalance in your union. This is what a real man looks like.

Is chocolate something she craves for during these times? Estrogen interacts with glucose leading to higher insulin levels. These higher insulin levels intensify sugar cravings. The results of these sugar cravings may be weight gain which further increases her estrogen levels. Fat cells produce estrogen leading to a downward spiral of weight gain. Research has shown that an overweight menopausal woman can produce as much estrogen as a thin woman who is pre-menopausal. Ref: http://www.ehow.com/about_5431853_symptoms-resulting-high-estrogen-levels.html

Knowledge sheds light to the dark areas of your life. The Father says, "My people are destroyed from lack of knowledge because you have rejected knowledge" {Hosea 4:6 NIV}. For this reason, you must apply everything that you have learned from this book. If you do not use the evidences that you now have, your relationship may be destroyed. What does your thoughtfulness show your woman? It displays your concern regarding her and your willingness to secure her peace and happiness. If she does not have peace and happiness, you do not have peace and happiness. Remember, if you are married, you both are one in the eyes of the Creator; therefore, whatever affects her affects you.

Once you know your woman well, you will settle conflicts before they even occur. I have defused countless arguments because I was in a protective mode and not in a defensive mode. A protective mode keeps the focus on your woman while a defensive mode puts the attention on you. A real man concentrates on his woman's needs as he serves in his role as her protector.

These are the three actions that you should perform for your woman when you sense she does not have comfort:

1.   pray for her;

2.   make her aware that you know something is wrong;

3.   reassure her by your actions.

First, prayer is the best course of action when you sense distress. Prayer is immediate communication with God. It gives the Lord permission to enter into the situation. He will reveal to you the concerns your woman is carrying and what you can do to restore her peace. We are spiritual beings having a physical experience; therefore, prayer heals and strengthens our spirit. When you do not know what is troubling her, plead her case before the Heavenly Judge. "For the Lord is our judge, the Lord is our lawgiver, the Lord is our king; it is he who will save us" {Isaiah 33:22NIV}. There are times that I do not know what is bothering my wife. At that point, I become her lawyer by presenting the evidence that I have to the Heavenly Judge. He knows and sees everything. He has already worked out a solution. Without my appeal, He cannot help my case. Remember this key phrase: God is not only your Father, but He is also your Father–in–law. He is the Father of your woman which makes Him your Father–in–law. He is concerned about His daughter, and He will give you all you need to restore her comfort, gladness, and strength.

Here is a prayer that I recite for my wife when her peace is missing:

Father, Your daughter is having some challenges at this moment, and I do not know what to do. I am praying to You because You know what to do and what I should be doing. I thank You in advance for hearing this prayer, and I thank You for providing me with the answer to this problem. I thank You in advance for removing all of the burdens concerning Your daughter. Thanks for filling her with Your comfort, in Jesus' name. Amen.

Secondly, make her aware that you know something is wrong, and you are going to do all you can to support her. This action is powerful since she knows you care. It proves you are paying close attention to her. When your woman is faced with difficulties, she may feel alone. However, she will fight her battles better knowing you are by her side. There is something about knowing you are not alone that empowers you.

Irritation is a sure sign of a lack of confidence, and I have learned that affection is a confidence builder. My steps towards rebuilding my wife's confidence include hugs, kisses, and reassuring words. I tell her, "You are not alone. I am here with and for you. What can I do to make matters better? Please tell me what is troubling you. We will fight this together." I call this attentive compassion. My conduct transforms the atmosphere.

If the issue remains after you have done all you can, maintain your diligence and trust that it will eventually leave. Maintaining your diligence does not mean you should become pushy. Instead, your persistence should represent security, reassurance, and comfort. Your attentiveness is a strong signal of the love you have for your woman. She will sense your consideration and be grateful for it. Remember, "Such love has no fear, because perfect love expels all fear. If we are afraid, it is for fear of punishment, and this shows that we have not fully experienced His perfect love" {1st John 4:18NLT}. Reassuring her with your words is a cake but reassuring her with your actions decorates the cake {icing and lit candles}.

Thirdly, the second you sense something is wrong with her, reassure her by your actions. Clean the house, give the kids a bath and put them to bed, cook her dinner, buy her some flowers, etc. Your actions are going to be appreciated and will remove the negative weights she is carrying. Your considerate behavior represents "SECURITY" which is very important to her. The sign of frustration means there was a breach in the security. When your actions remove the anxiety, her confidence will be recovered. Never underestimate the power of perfect love. One dose of perfect love makes all situations better.

You have the power to change the circumstances in your relationship. These steps secure the change. There is no act of kindness too big or too small because everything you do adds to your woman's security. Once these steps are taken, you will experience a very healthy relationship. It is all about going the extra mile to learn all you can about your woman. When you know your woman well, you become part of her solution and not part of her problem. You cannot go wrong when you extend your heart to your woman. Therefore, go the extra mile with her spiritually, and it will strengthen you both from the inside and out. Deeply understanding your woman makes her feel special. Who does not like to feel special? Your actions speak clearly; however, you should accompany them with the appropriate words. This one-two punch is sure to knockout the obstacles she may be facing. This is what a real man looks like and does.

The other day, my wife asked me to get a pair of shoes for her, but she gave me two options. If you were faced with these choices, which pair would you have gotten? I went for the first pair since I believed this selection was the one she favored the most. I was right. I know my woman well.

You will never know everything about your woman. As long as she lives, she is constantly evolving. The revelation here is you must evolve with her. Life is a journey. Enjoy the ride as you both discover each other's individualities. This approach bridges any gap and enforces unity. This knitting is the beauty of marriage and how the Creator designed for it to be. Take the time to learn as much as possible about your lady. Your efforts help you to help her. I believe a proactive approach is the best way to win future battles. Knowing your woman well is half of the battle. You must utilize what you have learned. By doing so, the relationship can then be all that the Lord desires for it to be. Your actions speak more to her than any words. So, be very attentive when it comes to her. Your attentiveness will please the Father, her, you, and your children. A real man knows his woman well because he views her as himself and treats her the way he would like to be treated. This is what a real man looks like and does.

Ladies, take the guessing game out of the equation. You must take the time to know your man well. This investment helps you to present your needs to him in a way he can understand eliminating unnecessary arguments and irritations. How many times have you said or thought to yourself, "He just does not understand me?" How frustrating is his lack of insight to you? What are you doing to remove the barriers? As my wife learned more about me, she changed how she presented her desires and concerns. For instance, she realizes that I am a very visual person. Therefore, if she wants to paint a room in our home, she knows I will better grasp her desire with a paint sample. Knowing your man well helps out with communication. We all learn differently, and we figure things out in our own special way. Some people learn best with their hands, others by reading, and several by demonstrations. For this reason, you need to know your man thoroughly. Do you know what his learning style is? Are you utilizing this style to get your point across? If not, you are not helping to avoid preventable disagreements that you may be experiencing.

Communicate! Find out what is the best way for you to present your interest to your man by having a simple conversation with him. This open discussion will clarify so much for you both and will certainly remove frustrations. Converse! Let him know you are asking him about his learning style because you want to maintain respect, peace, and love. Talk! Never assume anything. Ask him questions in regard to his likes and dislikes. Speak! Make an attempt to learn something new about him daily. We get comfortable after a while due to the amount of time we share with our mate. Do not get too comfortable. People are always changing. Knowing your man well is just another installment among many installments leading to a successful relationship.

Be sure you recognize his favorite color, his preferred restaurant, his desired food, his beloved song, his much loved movie, his chosen cologne, and his ideal designer. Learn what makes him laugh, what makes him cry, and what agitates him. Identify his passions, his number one vacation spot, his shoe size, and his favorite sport and team. Find out what is most important to him. It is essential that you to know as much as possible about your man.

Here is a prayer for you: Father, help me to understand "Justin" better. Help "Justin" to understand me better. I want to know him the way that I would like for him to know me. Let us experience the oneness that You designed for us to enjoy. Condition our hearts so we may go the extended mile for each other. Give us both the confidence to openly speak to each other regarding our needs. Thank You for the freedom that we are experiencing because the guessing games are over. I am thankful that we are effectively communicating and learning more about each other every day, in Jesus' name. Amen.

Reflection

Please take the time to journal your questions and comments as a powerful way to track your progress. These moments are when you take the time to reflect on what you have learned in this chapter and express your thoughts. What did you learn from this chapter? How well do you know your woman on a scale from one to ten? What should you do to learn more about her? What is the first thing you should do when you sense she is troubled? Did you take the time to find out when her menstrual cycle begins? What are you going to do for her during her menstrual cycle to make her feel better?

Many couples experience senseless frustrations because their level of communication is not what it should be. Talk to your woman constantly about her desires, likes, and dislikes. Effective communication helps you to know your woman well.

Here is a confession for you to pray: I am a man of excellence, and I excel in all that I do. I think big, and I get big results because I serve a big God. I go the extra mile with joy to honor God and my woman. I am a man of high standards just like Joseph, and I will maintain my standards no matter the circumstances. I am an overcomer; therefore, I succeed in all that I do. Thank You, Father, for helping me with this transformation. I am a real man, and I will demonstrate this stance daily, in Jesus' name. Amen.

See if you remember what you read in this chapter.

According to God, a person who is lacking knowledge is

_____ _____ _____ _____ _____ _____ _____ _____ _____.

A Real Man Is the Blender in His Blended Family

"The United States has the highest teen pregnancy rate in the industrialized world. The Center for Disease Control says that one-third of girls are pregnant before the age of 20. Teenpregnancy.org, a site managed by the National Campaign to Prevent Teen and Unplanned Pregnancy, states that there are "750,000 teen pregnancies annually. Eight in ten of these pregnancies are unintended and 81 percent are to unmarried teens." Ref: http://www.livestrong.com/article/12504-teen-pregnancy-rates-usa/#ixzz1xtJ4SNU6

Blended families are common, and once you add the divorce rate to this alarming statistic, the numbers are much greater. Blended families are found in every social and economic level. As I was growing up, I knew of only one family that was not blended. All of the other homes had either a stepmother or a stepfather in them. Based on the above statistics, it is likely for a man to inherit a stepchild. This man has to be skillful in order to deal with this challenging unification. I am speaking from experience. When I met my wife, she already had a child. A real man is the blender in his blended family.

God knew this issue would be a challenge. That is why He provided us with the fascinating story of Joseph and Mary to teach us how to effectively function in a blended family. Would you believe me if I told you Jesus was born and raised in a blended family? Joseph was not Jesus' natural father. Remember, Joseph and Mary was not intimate until after Jesus' birth. Mary was impregnated by the Holy Spirit; therefore, Joseph was Jesus' stepfather. "But as he was thinking this over, behold, an angel of the Lord appeared to him in a dream, saying, Joseph, descendant of David, do not be afraid to take Mary {as} your wife, for that which is conceived in her is of {from, out of} the Holy Spirit" {Matthew 1:20AMP}.

There are several trials that put a marriage or relationship to the test including infidelity, finances, and a blended family. My wife and I had quite a few problems in our relationship, but uniting our families was the biggest obstacle we faced. When we met, her daughter was quite young and an only child. She had never shared her mother with anyone before so she felt threatened believing I was occupying her space. Wars are fought over territory, and this situation was no different. Furthermore, I had three children of my own from two previous relationships joining this new family. Often, men date, fall in love, and marry a woman without courting the child as they should. The child is a major part of the woman rather than an additional portion. Quite a few men accept a fraction of the package and neglect the other part. This unwise choice leads to major conflicts. Once this stress occurs, the child feels insecure, vulnerable, and unwanted. You must accept and embrace the entire equation by including the child in activities. The closer the child feels to the new relationship, the better it will be for the transition. Unifying must be the focus.

Get to know your woman's children as you get to know her by inviting her children on the first couple of dates. If you buy the mother a gift, buy the children one also. If you pay the mother a compliment, pay the children one as well. As I stated earlier, you have to be skillful in order to deal with this challenging unification. Probably, the mother has always included her children in certain events. Follow her lead. If you do not, the children will feel threatened and isolated. No one wants to feel this way. You should extend yourself by displaying commitment and security. If commitment and security is good for the mother, commitment and security is good for the children.

How do you think the children would feel if you planned a date with them only? How do you think the children would feel if you called them after school and expressed your thoughtfulness? For instance, "How did you do on your test? Can I help you with anything? Can I take you to practice today? Can I help you study for your next exam?"

A blended family is not easy. As you are gaining the mother's trust, you also want to gain the trust of her children. Get rid of the word "stepchild" as this word adds even more pressure to the blending. This word causes division and tension when you want to introduce as much inclusion as possible. My wife and I learned during pre-marriage counseling that the word "stepchild" is not in the Bible, and God does not view children in this manner. In the eyes of the Creator, the children are yours. He expects for you to treat them as such. We do not use the word "stepchild" but refer to them as "our children." I do all I can to make this unified family function beautifully.

I pray aloud for our children based on their ages from the oldest to the youngest. I pray for my wife's daughter who is now "our daughter" second. My actions make her feel included which results in harmony in our household. How do you think she would feel if I added her name last? It is all about security. She appreciates being included in the middle of the relationship instead of being added to the end of it.

Are you planning to get married? If you are, explain the purpose of marriage to the children, and discuss the importance of this sacred unity. After sharing the importance of marriage, ask for the children's blessings and permission. I asked my wife's daughter for her blessings and permission and with a great big smile, she said, "Yes." You can make the transition smoother by involving the children in the wedding plans. My wife's daughter was included in our wedding plans, and she was empowered because her feelings were considered. This decision was a great way to ease any anxieties. At the reception, I danced with my wife's daughter after I danced with my wife. If I could go back in time, I would have recited separate vows to her and even given her a ring. If you want to win your woman's heart and gain her respect and trust, treat her children the way you would like for your children to be treated. Let her know how much you care about her children. Show her you are eager to fill any voids that her children may have in their lives. This is what a real man looks like and does.

Some men do not like their future stepchildren. This feeling creates an unhealthy environment and is very harmful for the relationship. It is better to keep the waters calm instead of causing waves. If this feeling pertains to you, remember it is a package deal. I know that a blended family can be very challenging. At times, I did believe I could not handle the pressures, and we even discussed going our separate ways. I am so glad I accepted ownership of the entire package that God had entrusted to me. The merger was one of the ways that I learned about dedication, love, and understanding. I had to humble myself for the sake of my marriage, and in the process, I was gaining "our daughter's" trust.

In a blended family you have different personalities and attitudes; therefore, it is your job to set the tone in your home. This unification is impossible without God. For this reason, He gave us the road to follow in this amazing story. Once Jesus is in the household, blended families will succeed. Was He not in the household with Joseph and Mary? Did their relationship not succeed? Once Jesus is allowed in your home, everything works as it should. You cannot rely on your intellect when it comes to a blended family. Your intelligence will not solve the problems. When a person is acting improperly, there is an internal issue that needs to be addressed. Your mind cannot grasp this truth. It always focuses on the surface. You have to deal with this matter from the spirit. Jesus is the one who can get to a person's heart and turn it around. "The king's heart is in the hand of the Lord, like the rivers of water; He turns it wherever He wishes" {Proverbs 21:1NKJV}. Until I incorporated Jesus, everything I tried during the merger failed. Honestly, the merger was stressful. However, the Mediator firmly held our marriage and family together. Thank You, Lord!

Once I submitted completely to God, all of our personalities and attitudes blended. You are the leader of your home, but you must submit to your Leader in order to properly lead your family. You have to be a strong follower of Christ to be a reliable guide for your wife and children. Introduce His views in your home daily, and your family will blend effectively.

A real man is the blender in his blended family. He brings all of the right fruits into his home unifying everyone. Here are the fruits you need to bring into your household daily: "But the fruit of the {Holy} Spirit {the work which His presence within accomplishes} is love, joy {gladness}, peace, patience {an even temper, forbearance}, kindness, goodness {benevolence}, faithfulness, Gentleness {meekness, humility}, self-control {self-restraint, continence}. Against such things there is no law {that can bring a charge}" {Galatians 5:22-23AMP}. My wonderful friend, Audrey Michael, shared this thought with me, "A blended family is like a smoothie. With the blender's help, a strawberry, banana, apple, mango, ice, and juice become one. You cannot tell the strawberry from the banana." This mixture comes together once the blended family is functioning God's way. Notice, the word "smooth" makes up the word "smoothie." When something is smooth, it is free from unevenness. A real man frees his blended family from all unevenness. Praise the Lord! We were able to add to our blended family with the birth of our daughter, Skyy.

This world is like a candy store. It has many different flavors. So, why do we reject the differences of others? People fail in society because they refuse to merge with others. If you are not able to blend inside of your home, you will have difficulties blending outside of your home. Remember, whatever impacts you internally will also impact you externally. Turn on the power within you, and unify your family. You can do it as Joseph did.

Ladies, if you are in a blended family, help your man with the merger. Let your man know the importance of inclusion as it pertains to your children. Never exclude the truth that you all are a package deal. Some women fall deeply in love with a man and forget about their children. Do not become so consumed in the man of your dreams that you neglect your children. If you do, your dreams will become a nightmare. Remember, a real man needs to be responsible for all of you, not just a part of you. Let him share in the responsibility of raising your children. You know the saying, "It takes a village to raise a child." You plus him equals the village.

You must display a united front at all times when your children are around representing the strong family unit they need. Eat dinner together, pray together, and make time for talking and listening to each other. As you and your man display consistent unity, your children will understand the importance of the family structure. Also, let your man know he is vital in the raising of your children by including him in the decision-making process. Try not to make a decision without first asking for his opinion. Inclusion works for him as well. I felt useful when my wife included me in the decisions regarding "our daughter," and I felt left out during the times that she excluded me.

You both should avoid discussing issues in front of the children, especially if they are rebellious towards the relationship. You are not always going to agree with each other, but the last

222

thing you want to display is division. Even if you both are divided behind closed doors, you must always show unity when the children are around. Children are very crafty. If they sense discord, they will utilize it to their advantage causing more problems than you know. Always discuss difficult topics among yourselves, and once a decision is made, remain united in their presence. The man is the blender in the blended family, and the woman is the cup holding the smoothie.

Here is a prayer for you: Father, help "Mario" and I with our blended family. Give us the patience to deal with all that comes with this merger. Supply us with wisdom and understanding during trying times. Bless our children with peace, speak to their hearts, and let them know that they are important to us. Let Your love be the ruling force that fills our home. Teach "Mario" how to be the blender in this blended family. I am grateful that "Mario" demonstrates the fruits of love, joy, peace, patience, kindness, goodness, faithfulness, gentleness, and self-control. I am so thankful for the example You have given us through this amazing story. Just like Joseph and Mary, we give Jesus access to all of our hearts and home. Because of Your guidance, we are becoming more of a family every day, and I am thankful for our unity, in Jesus' name. Amen.

Reflection

Please take the time to journal your questions and comments as a powerful way to track your progress. These moments are when you take the time to reflect on what you have learned in this chapter and express your thoughts. What did you learn from this chapter? What steps are you going to take to represent a blender in your blended family? Have the children offended you? Have you forgiven them? Do you think you can have a healthy relationship if you do not forgive them? What are you doing to protect your woman from the stress of the merger? Do you treat all of the children equally? Do you include them in some of the activities that you plan with your woman? Do they know you care about them? How do you display security to the children? What is your job as the blender in the family?

Here is a confession for you to pray: I am a man of excellence, and I excel in all that I do. I think big, and I get big results because I serve a big God. I go the extra mile with joy to honor God and my woman. I am a man of high standards just like Joseph, and I will maintain my standards no matter the circumstances. I am an overcomer; therefore, I succeed in all that I do. Thank You, Father, for helping me with this transformation. I am a real man, and I will demonstrate this stance daily, in Jesus' name. Amen.

See if you remember what you read in this chapter.

When something is smooth, what is it free from?

____ ____ ____ ____ ____ ____ ____ ____ ____ ____.

You are the leader; therefore, blend it all together. Joseph did it and with God's help, you can also.

Which Man Will You Become?

This book is dedicated to teaching you how to become a real man. However, you will never be a perfect man no matter how hard you try. We are spiritual beings having a physical experience, and there is nothing perfect about the physical side of life. Professional bodybuilders dedicate their entire lives to the art of bodybuilding, and yet, they are never fully satisfied with their bodies. They always see at least one area that they believe can be improved. The more time they invest in perfecting their body, the more their weaker part stands out. They spend endless hours lifting weights, running on a treadmill, and visualizing perfection, and at the end of the day, they are still not fully satisfied with what they see. If everything was perfect, where would there be room for improvement? It is the beauty of life that we have the opportunity to improve ourselves if we so desire. However, perfection eludes us.

In 1911, a magazine published an article on the White Star Line's sister ships, Titanic and Olympic. The editorial described the construction of the ships and concluded that the Titanic was practically unsinkable. When asked if the Titanic was really unsinkable, "God himself could not sink this ship" was the answer given by a deck hand. We all know what happened to this perfectly built ship. God did not sink it but an iceberg did. There is nothing we can construct in the physical sense that can be labeled perfect. All the money in the world cannot build a perfect ship. The tangible side of life is controlled by our senses, and as you well know, there is nothing perfect about our senses. They are ruled by what we see, hear, touch, smell, and taste. To put it simply, the human aspect has limitations and boundaries.

"I cannot respond the way Joseph did. That was Joseph not me. Let me put this book down because this story is not real. No man can live this way." If these thoughts are something you said to yourself, I agree with you one hundred percent. None of these accomplishments are possible to the physical man without God's help. You must strive for excellence and not for perfection in order to experience what Joseph experienced.

Striving for perfection will only frustrate you. Strive for excellence instead. You can become a man of excellence. You will never achieve perfection in this world; however, you can most certainly achieve excellence. You will make mistakes at times, but the mistakes are minimized when God is your pilot. Unlike the tangible world, there are no limitations or boundaries here because the mindset of excellence focuses on faith, and faith is the place of unlimited possibilities.

A basketball player explores his potential as he attempts to minimize his mistakes. Even if he shoots one thousand free throws a day and makes nine hundred and ninety-nine of them, he will eventually miss one; however, he continues to practice. He is attempting to minimize his misses and maximize the level of his success. There is no success without constant training. Constant training leads to excellence, and ultimately, he will be rewarded because of his efforts. His dedication grants him championships, fame, and wealth. The moment that you acquire excellence, a wonderful relationship with God, a fruitful relationship with your woman, and a great bond with your children will be your reward.

The average player focuses on the bad plays and the mistakes he has made. The player of excellence does the total opposite. He learns and is motivated by his mistakes. This player holds himself hostage after the game is over and drills in an empty stadium. This approach is the one to embrace. Learn from your mistakes. Utilize them as motivation towards a better you. According to the Lord, this attitude promotes a life of quality.

Once you make the investment that Joseph made, you will become a man of excellence. By no means was Joseph a perfect man; however, he excelled in character. He boldly went where the men of his days did not go by embracing Mary's unexpected pregnancy. You must be dedicated and determined to improve your life despite of the oppositions. It requires lots of practice to possess emotional, mental, and spiritual strength. Excellence is achieved by repetitious practice. It positions you on a stage all by yourself. People usually say, "Practice makes perfect." I disagree. You can practice something for countless hours and still have room for correction. I believe that practice breeds excellence. This belief removes the needless pressure of trying to obtain perfection.

You will fall down at times. Will you stay down or get back up? Men of excellence stumble and fall, but they learn and rise from every fall. Regaining their stance is not something they think about, but instead it is what they do. Throughout life, you will make mistakes; therefore, you must develop a champion's mentality. As you cultivate this way of thinking, you bounce back better and stronger from every fall. Willpower does not allow you to quit. Going the extra mile is the definition of determination. When most people say, "I can't" or "I am tired," the spirit of excellence says, "Let's go. I am well prepared for this obstacle. I am just getting started." Do you see the difference? When your woman knows you are a man of tenacity, she will love you even more deeply. Your character will inspire her to excel. Once I stepped my game up, my wife's game went to another level. The spirit of excellence makes everyone around you better. When you strive for excellence, your godly nature is leading the way, and your body follows. You must be fully persuaded to have your heart direct you instead of your senses. Allowing your heart to lead you helps you with your transformation. This change produces liberation. If freedom is absent, frustration is present and will hinder your efforts to become a real man.

The champion's mindset can be accomplished if you seriously desire it. As you step out of yourself and live for others, you will be living a well-fulfilled life. For instance, this book is my example of living for others because I wrote it with you in mind. I have a deep passion to help people achieve success in their relationships according to God's standards. Therefore, this book is my contribution to you and the world. When you decide to treat others the way you would like to be treated, you are well on your way to the winner's circle. Your dedication will change your life and have a positive influence on others.

If you live the way Jesus lived, you will experience spiritual perfection even though you are an imperfect being. Jesus was also a spiritual being having a physical experience; however, He lived by His Spirit and not by His flesh. You are not able to perfect your physical life, but you can certainly perfect your spiritual life even more. Your spirit is perfect, and it is always yearning for perfection. Jesus said, "Keep watch and pray, so that you will not give in to temptation. For the spirit is willing, but the body is weak!" {Matthew 26:41NLT}. Your inner man keeps you in alignment with the Lord which helps you to achieve excellence in the physical world and perfection in the spiritual world.

Like the basketball player, as you invest more time in improving your heart {spirit}, you will make fewer mistakes. Joseph lived from his heart; therefore, he exhibited self-control, amazing character, and wisdom. All of the principles found in this book are acquirable when you live from your heart. However, these values will escape you if you are living from your flesh because your flesh wages war against your heart. Success or failure is dependent upon the controlling forces of your life. Is your inner man or your outer man in control? Living internally is the only way to live. My senses led me in the wrong direction; however, my spirit steered me on the right path. In the beginning of this journey, I was worn down and frustrated. I was applying these spiritual principles to my natural mind, and I experienced nothing but defeat. Once I understood the difference between the inner man and the outer man, everything turned around for me. Truthfully, the results were instantaneous. Since the spirit is perfect, the spirit does not encounter defeat as it is ruled by the Lord. With the Creator, everyone succeeds.

Once you understand this truth, you will become the perfect lover of God by being obedient to His instructions. You will become the perfect lover of your woman by accepting responsibility and rapidly correcting your wrongs. You will become the perfect lover of your children by being the example of a real man. You will become the perfect lover of mankind by living according to these principles. "You, therefore, must be perfect {growing into complete maturity of godliness in mind and character, having reached the proper height of virtue and integrity}, as your heavenly Father is perfect" {Matthew 5:48AMP}.

This transformation does not mean you will not make mistakes or you will always say the right things. However, if you are out of alignment, honor immediately steers in the right direction. Honor is a driver bringing order, peace, and wisdom. Where will you allow honor to drive you? When will you allow honor to drive you? How often will you allow honor to drive you? Life is quite a road to travel, and if you are traveling without honor as your chauffeur, the journey is a long and weary. Honor has to be your driver. You are lost without this valuable guide. Honor has a navigation system that helps you to find the best way to your destination safe and sound.

Ladies, I encouraged you throughout this book to help your man with his transformation by applying the principles that you have learned. If you have been faithfully utilizing these principles and praying for him, you should be seeing the fruits of your efforts. Have you experienced personal changes after reading this book? What has improved about you the most? Who is benefiting from your improvements? Do you have more self-confidence? While you were focused and faithful to helping your man transform into a real man, you were being transformed into a "Real Woman." I am not saying you were not a real woman before you read this book. However, this transformation was not only for your man, but it was also for you. Everything you have endured throughout this process has rebuilt your foundation from the inside out. Look at yourself and ask what you see? Are you not thinking, acting, and speaking differently? Do you feel like your mind is renewed? Do you see relationships the way you once did? Do you understand love more deeply?

Even though we are at the end of this book, the writing continues from this point forward. There is a new chapter for the two of you to write. The new chapter is titled "A New Life." Your life, his life, and your journey together are a manuscript. Here are the questions you both need to answer: "What category of book are you two writing? Is it an amazing love story or a horror tale? Do people desire to read it or are they not interested in the storyline?" You both have the power to co-author a new narrative. Therefore, utilize what you have learned, inspire the world, and be the model couple for everyone who you meet. Your negative and positive experiences hold interest for many couples. You can powerfully help them with the same issues that you once had. Look for opportunities to help other men/women/couples who may be experiencing what you have experienced. Teach them "What Does A Real MAN Look Like?" Show them the steps that carved out the new and improved you. Does it make sense for you to be on the eighth floor while your mate remains on the ground level? Of course not! You both transitioned together. Take other people or couples on the elevator of your journey and show them how you both elevated as a couple.

This journey was an investment that you both made with and for each other. I know that it was well worth it. Now, your children are benefiting from a healthy home and family structure. Because you both were willing to take this journey as a team, your children now have the solid foundation needed to become productive adults. Do you see how your acts of love are now able to reach people who you may never meet? Your actions will live forever. Your children will pass on what they have learned to their children, and so on. Also, your children will be able to influence their friends with the seeds that you both have planted into their lives. Earlier in the book, I referred to "a cycle of continuous giving." Here is the cycle that you both have started.

Remember, an appropriate investment benefits everyone involved. You both made a wonderful investment in each other and for each other. The story of Mary and Joseph represents the greatest investment of all time. The Creator invested Himself by using a virgin {Mary} and a man of amazing standards {Joseph}. His investment resulted in the greatest creation this world has ever seen – JESUS! Jesus is God's perfect gift to the world. Those who accept Him will profit in this life and the life to come. For this reason, I repeatedly suggested throughout this book to include Him in your relationship. Jesus is the only perfect "MAN" who ever lived. He is able to perfect all imperfections in your life and union.

You both are growing together with your imperfections and perfectly loving each other through it all. This new outlook will have a positive impact on your children, family, and everyone you meet. People are going to admire the bond you two have. This admiration creates opportunities. Let them know about the "MAN" who forever changed your life – Jesus. As you perfect the love that you both have for each other, you are promoting God to the world. You may be the only sign of God a person sees. Represent Him well. Never stop displaying the passion of Christ for others. Never stop going the extra mile. Never stop praying for each other. Never underestimate the power of your prayers.

Here is a prayer for you: Father, I understand we are not perfect; however, I am asking You to continuously perfect our hearts towards You and each other. Give us a strong desire to please You daily. Grant us a deep passion to honor one another as we honor You. I am very grateful that we are displaying the spirit of excellence through our words, actions, and attitudes. I am so thankful that our standards are of Heaven and not of earth. Thank You for allowing us the opportunity to spread Your love to others. Thank You for helping us to excel in all that we do. I am glad that we are pleasing You as we pursue the spirit of excellence, in Jesus' name. Amen.

Reflection

Please take the time to journal your questions and comments as a powerful way to track your progress. These moments are when you take the time to reflect on what you have learned in this chapter and express your thoughts. What did you learn from this chapter? Were you the type of man who attempted to reach perfection? Did this chapter clarify the difference between excellence and perfection? Do you now have a sense of relief or freedom? What are you going to do when you fall down? How much time are you going to spend focusing on your mistakes? How much time are you going to spend focusing on the solutions? What is your favorite chapter in this book? Why is it your favorite chapter? What is the greatest lesson you learned from this book? How are you going to share this lesson with others?

Here is a confession for you to pray: I am a man of excellence, and I excel in all that I do. I think big, and I get big results because I serve a big God. I go the extra mile with joy to honor God and my woman. I am a man of high standards just like Joseph, and I will maintain my standards no matter the circumstances. I am an overcomer; therefore, I succeed in all that I do. Thank You, Father, for helping me with this transformation. I am a real man, and I will demonstrate this stance daily, in Jesus' name. Amen.

See if you remember what you read in this chapter.

What does the spirit of excellence focus on?

_____ _____ _____ _____ _____.

INVITATION

I was once in the music industry, and I lived the life that many people dream of living. I met the biggest stars, and I enjoyed all of the perks that came with these associations. Everyone I met plus all that I experienced does not compare to the MAN I met in 2001. I met a MAN then who taught me everything I know today. This MAN accepted me for who I was. He did not judge or condemn me. In reality, He was the first MAN who expressed His unconditional love for me. This MAN cherished me when no one else did. He gave me a chance when everyone else gave up on me. He gave me hope when I felt hopeless. He clarified to me, "What Does A Real MAN Look Like!" He showed me how to be a good husband and father. I was lost, and He found me. There is nothing you have done wrong that He will not forgive. All you have to do is sincerely confess your sins to God. "If we confess our sins, he is faithful and just and will forgive us our sins and purify us from all unrighteousness" {1st John 1:9NIV}.

If you want to meet this MAN, He is ready to meet you. He has been waiting for this moment your entire life. His name is Jesus. The introduction is very simple. All you have to do is repeat this prayer, and He will enter into your heart. He will do for you what He has done for me and countless others. Are you ready to experience the best relationship in the world? Are you ready to experience a transformation that will forever change your life for the better?

Read this prayer aloud

Jesus, I do not know You, but I am ready to meet You at this moment. Come into my heart, and give me the changes that Enrique describes. I am ready to live for You and follow Your instructions. I trust You. I believe in You. Forgive me of my sins. Cleanse me from the inside out. Give me a new heart. Help me to reprogram my mind. Teach me how to live the way You desire for me to live. Thank You for dying for my sins, for forgiving me, and for cleansing me from all unrighteousness. I accept the freedom You give me. I will not hold onto my past. I am now embracing my future with You. I believe you are the Son of God. I believe in Your death, burial, and resurrection. I thank You, Jesus, for raising me up from a place of death and for giving me eternal life, in Your name I pray. Amen.

IF YOU RECITED THIS PRAYER, WELCOME TO THE FAMILY. YOUR LIFE IS NO LONGER THE SAME. YOUR NEW FAITH IS A PERSONAL RELATIONSHIP BETWEEN YOU AND GOD. LIKE ALL RELATIONSHIPS, TIME DETERMINES HOW FAR IT GOES. INVEST AS MUCH TIME AS POSSIBLE IN IT, AND YOU ARE GOING TO EXPERIENCE THE BEST FRIENDSHIP THAT YOU HAVE EVER HAD. PRAY CONSTANTLY, READ THE BIBLE REGULARLY, AND SPEAK TO GOD ALWAYS. FINALLY, JOIN A CHURCH WHICH EMPHASIZES THE BIBLE. GOD LOVES YOU MORE THAN YOU WILL EVER KNOW. GOD BLESS YOU!